WHO STOLE THE SOUL?

THE WEAPONIZATION OF HIP HOP

A Historical & Sociological Perspective

BERNARD O. CREAMER JR.

ACKNOWLEDGMENTS

Much gratitude and respect to my immediate and extended tribe…much love and reverence to our dope ancestry…huge shoutout to the Culture that is hip hop and all of those who have poured into it with the respect due to it...
ONE.

CONTENTS

INTRODUCTION

'Who Stole the Soul?' is the title to one of my favorite Public Enemy jams. The first verse of the song touches on the exploitation of Black musicians by America's music industry. The exploitation and manipulation of Black music artists is a longstanding American historical reality. It is tradition. It has never not been the case. In many instances, we have seen where the messages of Black music and musicians were altered to suit the sensibilities of mainstream White audiences. In years past, they would replace pictures of Black musicians with pictures of White artists on album covers to render the visuals more palatable, to ensure a profit. Black artists rarely got their fair share of those profits. Many a Black rock and roll, country, blues, jazz, or rhythm and blues artist has seen their image and music "white-washed" and purged of its soul to suit the majority White population of this country. Oftentimes, Black musicians fought the alteration of their art and identities, resulting in them being "white-listed" and rendered unemployed. Too often, Black musicians would succumb to the allure of commercial success, fame, and fortune, and lose themselves altogether. Soul music minus the soul. Hip Hop wasn't immune to this same co-option and control

Hip Hop began as a spark ignited by the environment and oppression Black youth found themselves ensconced in during the 1970s. It was an outlet to air their thoughts that blossomed into a full-fledged mega-medium. Hip Hop was initially employed to work out conflicts and differences between neighborhood factions of Black youth, verbal sparring. It was a way to vent on the realities of Black people living on the edge and being pushed to the margins of a society that has no allegiance to them. Hip Hop was the manifestation of artistic genius that featured potent painted mosaics on walls, and the limber, athletic contortions of break dancers on cardboard pallets. It was poetry set to clever loops and break beats. It provided the vibe for parties packed with teens and twenty-somethings dancing rhythmically to the music of our elders and ancestry, re-mastered and remixed to suit the rebellious spirit of a new generation. Hip Hop was the manifestation of a Black generation awakening.

Hip Hop evolved to become our platform to speak on Black marginalization and the need for revolution. It was the much-needed jolt to awaken a mass of people rocked to sleep by a previous decade's worth of Blaxploitation flicks. At its inception, many of the genre's major acts saturated the soundscape with music of inspiration, encouragement, enlightenment, and a staunch rejection of systemic oppression. Black youth were learning and then teaching one another through Hip Hop. The youth were growing empowered by knowledge of themselves, their culture, their history, and their ancestry. The foundation was being laid for Black kids to become Black adults who stood up to oppression and led their respective communities in positive directions. The very last thing the American establishment wants is an awakened population of Black people who know who we are, where we come from, our connections to other Black people around the globe, our own worth, and what we are entitled to as human beings. Something had to be done. Hip Hop was growing too powerful.

The weaponization of Hip Hop was America's answer to a Hip-Hop culture that was fortifying and cultivating the minds of young Black people. In the beginning, Hip Hop was a tool Black kids utilized to edify one another. It was eventually co-opted, controlled, and commercialized to be used as a weapon to debase those it initially helped to empower. What was thought to be a fad at first by record companies became a major platform used ingeniously by those who gave birth to it. Those who control the reigns to American society recognized Hip Hop's power and sought ways to not only douse its positive social potential, they also sought ways to profit from what those clever Black youth had created. The paradigm began to shift. Hip Hop gradually went from a meal that featured a main course of conscious songs and culturally grounded artists, to offerings that mostly promoted the glamorization of everything negative. Positive and conscious artists were relegated to an underground while those who promoted Black death, misogyny, materialism, criminal behavior, and irresponsible drug and alcohol use were paid well and heavily promoted by record companies. Hip Hop was corporatized and consolidated to become an industry that cared little about Black people or Black culture; the priority was profits. It is difficult to profit from, exploit, and manipulate a group of people who are both astute and culturally aware, so rampant ignorance was infused into what Black youth consumed musically to make the artists easier to use. Eventually, Hip Hop no longer belonged to Black people. It was owned by Jews/Europeans who decided what would be supplied, while at the same time, contriving a demand for what toxifies. The culture was devalued while huge record companies profited mightily from what remained. The shift that began in the late 80s has regressed into what presents itself today as Hip Hop, while retaining none of the components that served as its pillars at inception.

Progress?

In the beginning, Hip Hop was DJ'ing, break dancing, graffiti, lyricism, and dropping knowledge. Today, the Hip Hop being heavily promoted is the new minstrel show, a defiled Black culture. We are living many of the negative manifestations of this paradigm shift. The soul has been sucked out of Hip Hop and it has been re-fashioned as a weapon of toxic "propagandization."

There are many historical precedents that parallel what has occurred and what is occurring within Hip Hop culture. The most consistent theme sees the use of propaganda to help dehumanize certain groups of people. This dehumanization helps to open the door for the disrespect, mistreatment, incarceration, and eventual neutralization of the targeted group. The same use of negative propaganda also helps to dilute the pride, self-esteem, and self-respect of the targeted group consuming the massive doses of pointed and functional self-destructive images and messages. Those picked for purging are primed to no longer see value in themselves and they begin to no longer stand or make demands for power. What has happened in the past is happening now, the cyclical nature of history.

This sort of propaganda use for genocidal purposes has not been limited to Black people. Other groups have been victimized as well. The long-existing template is being reapplied. Negative propaganda primed the Jews for Hitler's "Final Solution" in the 1930s as Europe prepared for WWII. Jews were mass slaughtered after Hitler's propaganda machinery had rendered them sub-humans unworthy of existence. Now the same formula the Nazis used is being applied to Black people by Jews/Europeans. Black people in the United States and around the globe are being targeted with genocide through a multitude of methods. The media is just one front.

What is happening to Hip Hop culture in America is right in step with what has always occurred with organic cultural creativity. Someone finds a way to exploit that creativity for money and it is quickly commercialized and commoditized. America's economic ideology calls for it. America is governed by the economic ideology and system, capitalism, and its social stratifications are by-products, classes within a caste system. Within such a system, targeted groups of people are relegated to a bottom rung. Black people have manned that bottom rung since the birth of this nation. Capitalism's machinery and policies are employed in the interest of maintaining the debilitating divisions forged within it, inherent to it. The most powerful apparatus employed by this country's owners is its corporate media. The way information in the United States is dispensed and controlled is functionally linked to the status quo which sees the rich staying rich and the poor wanting more. The use of propaganda, disguised as Hip Hop, is helping to maintain the current status quo which sees Black people looking up, and for a way up. It's important to understand the use of all media, including Hip Hop music, to direct a society's agendas and priorities. America's agendas and priorities are being played out as policies that see Black people disenfranchised. Black people are disproportionately unemployed, impoverished, incarcerated, and killed in this country. This reality is not happenstance.

I love Hip Hop and have for decades, and I fully understand how powerful it is as a major component of Black culture. For Black people, Hip Hop is largely responsible for defining our self-image. It's largely responsible for determining who and what we value. It helps to establish our norms just as much or more than any other genre of music we presently consume. Hip Hop recently overtook rock and roll as the most engaged genre of music in America. There is no doubting its influence, especially its influence on those who it targets, Black people, especially young Black people. Irony is the fact that White kids are the majority consumers of Hip Hop. Population proportionality plays into this, but the truth is, White kids have always enjoyed the window seat that allows them that peek into what has come to be deemed "the 'hood". It provides them with a license to be Black without having to be Black.

The goal of this book is to hopefully shed light on what I find to be important but not often discussed historical, sociological, and scientific concepts related to the powerful medium that is Hip Hop. We have an inherent responsibility to protect Black culture and to understand how our culture influences our young. Our culture is supposed to help nourish and cultivate us, not toxify, and destroy us. My hope is that the information contained within this book helps us to understand how Hip Hop culture is being manipulated and controlled in order to sustain our marginalization. More importantly, I hope the information serves as a springboard to more potent and sustained activism around the subject. No one can or will protect Black culture but Black people. Hip Hop is ours.

I have infused a lot of pointed perspectives into this book on the subject of Hip Hop, not to disparage it or the current artists, but to help call awareness to our need to protect it. Hopefully, it will be viewed as constructive and coming from a place of love. I have been a lover of Hip Hop since I was 14 years old. I am a product of the genre. I do not see a lot of value in placing the bulk of the blame for hip hop's current state on today's rappers because I have never seen value in hammering kids with condescension. Yes, we need to hold our youth accountable the same way we hold the adults accountable who misrepresent us or our culture. It must be noted though that, as adults, we are collectively responsible for guiding our youth. Wherever they wind up is the result of what we have or haven't done. It's on the Black village to empower them. We have largely allowed American society to sculpt and mold our kids. Many wind up very rough around the edges while being cast out to society's edges. We have left our youth exposed to be attacked psychologically, unshielded by the cultivation we're responsible for imparting. The adults are fully complicit in whatever waywardness our kids exhibit. That maladjustment and misdirection is on us. The minds of our youth are being manipulated by mass media. The onus of protecting their minds is OUR responsibility.

Through this book, I hope to shed light on the reality that is a very functional and deliberate paradigm shift. As hip hop's creators, Black people did not initiate this shift, the new landlords did. Its Jewish/European controllers did. Hip Hop has grown, but in what direction, and at whose expense? Some Black kids are getting paid but who's paying the cost for what's being promoted? Hip Hop grew up and lost its soul. Collectively, Black people are the curators of Black culture. If we're not protecting what's ours, who is? Everything popularized, promoted, and profited from in the larger American culture is not positive. Much of what America's corporate media popularizes, promotes, and profits from is poisonous, especially to those not possessing power. Black youth have gone from being the owners and major players in the Hip Hop game to being well-compensated pawns. Hip Hop is just a microcosm of the macro though. It isn't just Black youth who are subject to this sort of exploitation. The same dynamic applies within every American entity or institution we find ourselves employed. The lack of control over our own affairs is killing us. We are merely surviving at this juncture, but if we are looking to thrive again, we need to take back control of our culture and restore it back to its vibrant, creative, uplifting, nourishing, and empowering ways, back to when it benefitted us, as our own culture is supposed to.

CHAPTER 1
Relevant Terms

CULTURE - the sum of attitudes, customs, and beliefs that distinguish one group of people from another. *Culture* is transmitted through language, material objects, rituals, institutions, and art from one generation to the next.

People are defined by their culture. A people's culture is not only a direct reflection of who they are, it is the mechanism through which a group of people relate to and interact with one another. Through culture, norms and acceptable/unacceptable behaviors are established. Culture is a gauge that measures the health and sickness within a community of people. Culture is the means through which standard operating procedures are passed through each successive generation.

The most important component in any culture is language. Communication, both oral and written, is what facilitates our connections with one another. Among the most potent mediums is music. Music helps convey self-image standards, and it's generally more powerful than other mediums because the messages are accompanied by rhythmic wavelengths and vibrations which lend to the intended messages resonating both consciously and subconsciously. For example, a lot of K-12 teachers have begun to incorporate Hip Hop music into their curricula as a means of getting the information being taught to "stick". Children are having an easier time recalling lessons when they are accompanied by a catchy tune. We consciously and subconsciously absorb messages the exact same way through music played over the radio. With its popularity, Hip Hop has provided the template for how Africans and others engage one another from day to day. The genre has also done a masterful job of molding self-image. Hip Hop has the power to augment Black culture for good and bad.

MEDIA - the main means of communication (especially television, radio, newspapers, and the internet) regarded collectively.

MEDIA LITERACY - Possessing knowledge of what media is, the various mediums, its functions, its controllers, and the behavioral and psychological manifestations of its consumption.

PROPAGANDA - information, especially of a biased or misleading nature, used to promote or publicize a particular political cause or point of view.

SUBLIMINAL MESSAGE - any sensory stimuli below an individual's threshold for conscious perception.

GENOCIDE - the deliberate killing of a large group of people, especially those of a particular ethnic group or nation.

MISOGYNY - the hatred of women.

DEHUMANIZE - to deprive of positive human qualities.

DESENSITIZE - to cause someone to react less or be less affected by something.

DEMONIZE - to portray as wicked or threatening.

CONSUMERISM - the belief that it is good to spend a lot of money on goods or services.

MATERIALISM - a tendency to consider material possessions and physical comfort as more important than spiritual values.

CAPITALISM - an economic and political system in which a country's trade and industry are controlled by private owners for profit, rather than by the state.

CASTE SYSTEM - a social system in which people are grouped in hierarchical social categories, the most common being upper, middle, and lower classes.

STATUS QUO - the current situation; the way things are now.

SUBJUGATION - to defeat and gain control of someone by the use of force.

SOCIALIZATION - the process by which individuals acquire the knowledge, language, social skills, and values to conform to the norms and roles required to integrate into a group or community.

WESTERNIZATION - the social process of becoming familiar with or converting to the customs and practices of Western civilization.

WEAPONIZATION - to convert to use as a weapon.

13th Amendment of the United States Constitution - (Section 1) - "Neither slavery or involuntary servitude, EXCEPT AS A PUNISHMENT FOR CRIME WHEREOF THE PARTY SHALL HAVE BEEN DULY CONVICTED, shall exist within the United States. . ."

Every single one of the above terms is extremely relevant

in any analysis of media and the way it is employed in a society. This book centers on Hip Hop culture so it's very important to understand these terms in relation to the way the genre of music is wielded as either a tool or a weapon by those who control it. I emphasized culture by providing a lengthy definition of it because it is paramount that we understand how important Black culture is to Black people. We cannot afford to allow others, especially those who don't have our best interests at heart, to own, control, and disseminate Black images, narratives, and stories. In order for a people to have some measure of control over how they are portrayed in mass media. They must have ownership and control of major mediums and platforms that enable them to shape their own perceptions, definitions, and identities. It's important for Black people to own platforms such as radio, TV, movie studios and distribution, magazines, and social media. At present, that ownership doesn't exist as much as needed which results in overall negative depictions of Black people and Black culture. Most of the terms listed above are associated with what transpires when we do not own the major conduits of our culture. They will be employed further as we delve deeper.

CHAPTER 2
Genesis

1520 Sedgwick Avenue, The Bronx, New York

(Al Pereira/Getty Entertainment/Getty Images)

In the early 1970's, a Jamaican disc jockey known as Kool Herc moved from Kingston, Jamaica to New York City's Bronx borough. He started hosting parties in the recreation room of his building on Sedgwick Avenue. He spun music attempting to employ a Jamaican style which involved reciting freestyle rhymes over the dubbed versions of reggae songs. "Dubbed" refers to the removal of the song's original words. At the time, New York's Bronx partiers weren't really vibing with reggae music so instead of placing his own vocals over reggae dubs, he placed them over the instrumental or percussion sections of more popular music. The breaks in these songs were usually pretty short so he figured out a way to extend them with the use of two turntables and a sound mixer. He'd play two of the same records simultaneously and then extend the breaks by switching from one record to the other, starting at the beginning of the break each time and using the mixer to cross-fade to the other record each time the break ended. Certain "break beats" became popular after some time and the more popular rappers would want to rap on them. Eventually, albums were pressed out featuring nothing but break beats, often cleverly sampled mainstream music. Hip Hop was conceived.

DJ Kool Herc (musicorigins.org, 2020)

The seeds were planted for Hip Hop to grow into a powerful subculture, ushered in by a Bronx neighborhood of Black youth looking for a release. Like many Black youth today, a lot of Black 70's kids found themselves dealing with poverty, gangs, violence, ineffective schools, drugs, family dysfunction, and a society that appeared to not care about any of it. They released themselves at parties where they danced to party jams and enjoyed the spirit of a tribe's love. The dj was the motor of the party and the music served as the fuel. Talented and creative djs like Kool Herc, Afrika Bambaataa, Grand Wizzard Theodore, and Grandmaster Flash provided the soundscapes as rappers tested their lyrical dexterity riding the bridges provided by these turntable masters. After a while, there were djs and rappers who would battle one another taking the parties to another level. Among the first and most famous rap battles featured Kool Moe Dee going against Busy Bee. Later Kool Moe Dee would also battle LL Cool J. Legendary duels. These rap battles were a welcome alternative to the physical altercations that often resolved conflicts in the 'hood, often with deadly consequences. In March of 1979, The Fatback Band, featuring King Tim III, became the first commercial release of a rap record. Sugar Hill Gang's *Rapper's Delight* was released in September of that same year. Hip Hop became "official".

At its roots, Hip Hop featured djs, lyricists, graffiti artists, and break dancers. Not long afterwards, the impartation of knowledge was infused. If you weren't proficient in one or more of these components, you couldn't call yourself Hip Hop. Pretenders were exposed and purged quickly. My favorite rap groups included djs and rappers who did party music, but also dropped much-needed cultural awareness. Rap styles and patterns gradually grew more complex. Hip Hop djing and producing were talents only a relative few possessed in the beginning.

Hip Hop was blossoming into a full-fledged culture. America's music industry didn't see Hip Hop as a genre that would have any real staying power, it was mostly dismissed as a fad. Not only did Hip Hop grow, it went global. Acts were signed, records were sold, groups were touring, and the artists and others involved were getting paid. When it first took off, rap was safe from culture vultures. It wasn't seen as a viable commodity by those who have historically taken a liking to co-opting and exploiting Black creativity and culture for profit. Genres such as Rock and Roll, Jazz, Blues, Rhythm and Blues, and House music all began organically. All of these musical forms were created, owned, and embraced by African people. They were eventually commercialized, diluted, and profited from by people beyond the culture. Hip Hop would eventually experience the same.

Sugar Hill Records was created in 1979 and was among the first labels to specialize in Hip Hop. The label was owned by Joe and Sylvia Robinson. Sylvia Robinson was also an artist on the label that included the Sugar Hill Gang rap group who released the immensely successful "Rappers Delight". At first, the Robinsons welcomed a partner in Morris Levy who was a major funder, but once the label took off, they bought him out. Problems later arose for Sugar Hill when they signed a major distribution deal. Large media corporations were gradually easing their hands into the cookie jar that was a burgeoning and profitable music form.

In 1984, Def Jam Records was born out of a partnership between Rick Rubin and Russell Simmons. They went on to sign some of Hip Hop's most successful acts including LL Cool J. Their situation became muddled, when, like Sugar Hill Records, they signed with a major distributor. Major distributors are companies such as Columbia, Universal, and Sony who are primarily interested in profits. Distributors open doors for artists through heavy promotion and getting the artists' music into stores. They don't appreciate Hip Hop as the cultural jewel it is, they see it as a medium to be monetized. These distribution deals marked the beginning of Hip Hop's major paradigm shift. We were losing ownership of the beautiful baby we gave birth to.

As teens in the 80's, we saw some of the changes occurring, but we were quick to chalk them up to petty differences between our favorite group's members. The distributors who now owned the record labels were seeking to maximize their bottom lines. Djs were quickly being replaced by producers who made beats for entire rosters of label artists. Groups were divided and the more profitable members would eventually be signed, leaving the other group members behind; this should sound familiar to fans of old school R&B. The content, substance, and messages of the music began to matter less, making way for emphasis on the beats. Break dancing and graffiti, as components of Hip Hop, had all but evaporated. Knowledge of self, as a major ingredient, gave way to materialism, misogyny, thug life, and abject ignorance. Hip Hop was gradually whittled down to one piece, the lyricist. With many of the new lyricists, the industry placed the focus on some contrived persona versus actual talent.

At the beginning of Hip Hop's commercialization, we still had conscious rappers and rap groups that were mainstream. The more carnal and profane elements of Hip Hop remained underground, adorned with parental advisory stickers. The parental advisory sticker was first placed on compact discs in 1985. The first artist blessed with the designation was Ice-T. Artists earn the distinction by putting out music that contains strong language, depictions of violence, sex, or substance abuse. Initially, conscious acts rarely contained any of the aforementioned themes. Conscious acts included Brand Nubian, KRS-1, Public Enemy, A Tribe Called Quest, Queen Latifah, MC Lyte, X-Clan, De La Soul, Black Star, The Coup, Common, and even Ice Cube before he reverted back to his NWA roots. These acts crafted the cuts that dominated the party scene and our consumption as Hip Hop heads. Their music uplifted, inspired, encouraged, and empowered us while entertaining us. There were quite a few acts that were considered a bit grimier that spoke to the realities of the streets, which was reality for many, but these artists and "gangster rap" weren't quite the status quo yet. Schoolly D, Ice-T, and Just-Ice were a few of the first rappers to populate the gangster rap genre. Boogie Down Production's *Criminal Minded* with KRS-1 blessing Scott La Rock's hard-hitting beats was released in 1987 and it featured many elements of that street realism that came to eventually rule the Hip Hop landscape. Eventually, that parental advisory sticker began to become synonymous with all Hip-Hop music. The parental advisory sticker never became much of a factor in regard to helping parents shield their impressionable children from certain edgier themes. It more so served as a means of protecting the record companies from liability in regard to the music being targeted at kids that contained those "adult themes". Today, the sticker is totally obsolete as most kids and adults download or stream their favorite artists from digital platforms.

Hip Hop is a major piece of my childhood and young adult years. Along with Hip Hop, House music fed me both mentally and spiritually. I was introduced to both genres in my early teens. I credit the birth of House music, Hip Hop, and the release of *Star Wars* in 1977 as being among the most nostalgic and euphoric reference points in my younger years.

Hip Hop had a myriad of influences prior to its actual inception that include the Black church, old school Black comedians, and Native African griot tradition. Hip Hop and House music were both influenced by the dying era of Disco. Disco was fast paced, decadent, flashy and it provided the atmosphere for many a ritzy, limited access night club. Most notably, Disco appealed to two marginalized segments of the American population, Blacks and gays. In addition, it was perceived as anti-Rock and Roll which naturally didn't appeal to the European majority of America. Disco had to be killed, and so it was, quite unceremoniously. The births of both House Music and Hip Hop were spirited and rebellious reactions to Disco being faded out. The death of Disco laid the foundation for both of these future giants, Hip Hop and House music. The foundation for Hip Hop in New York was laid a couple of years before the birth of House music in Chicago in 1977. Being from Chicago, I was introduced to House music a few years before I met Hip Hop. Much respect to Hip Hop's founder, Kool Herc, and House music's father, Frankie Knuckles for blessing us with these sonic juggernauts. I had to make mention of House music because my love for it matches my affinity for Hip Hop. However, the focus of this book is Hip Hop. Maybe House music will get a manuscript from me later on down the road.

Written by Donna Summer/Giorgio Moroder (1977). *I Feel Love.* (Donna Summer). From the album *I Remember Yesterday.* Los Angeles, California: Casablanca Records.

Written by Donna Summer/John Barry (1978). *Theme From the Deep (Down, Deep Inside)* (Donna Summer) From the album *Live and More.* Los Angeles, California: Casablanca Records.

Written by Bryan Walton (Jamie Principle) (1986). *Your Love.* (Jamie Principle/Frankie Knuckles). From the 12" *Your Love.* Chicago, Illinois: Trax Records.

Besides Disco, Hip Hop had other influences. Among the more potent influences contributing to the birth of Hip Hop was Melvin Van Peeble's movie, *Sweet Sweetback's Baadasssss Song.* His blockbuster 1971 movie garnered him millions of dollars while defying Hollywood's owners displeased with a storyline that saw a Black man rise above his circumstances and win, defeating "the man". Mr. Van Peebles wrote, directed, produced, edited, starred in, and arranged the soundtrack for the movie. *Sweetback's* success influenced European/Jewish vultures of Black culture to begin making movies that came to be known as Blaxploitation movies. The term Blaxploitation encompasses the fact that these movies were targeted to Black audiences and featured the consistent theme of Blacks battling the White establishment. They also included mostly Black actors/actresses who, through seedy roles and characters, reinforced negative stereotypes about Black people. The movies also contained gratuitous amounts of violence, much of it directed at one another. As the genre's name suggests, Black people were being exploited through these movies. Hip Hop would later get its turn to mirror the exact same exploitation.

Blaxploitation movies featured colorful, charismatic characters like Foxy Brown and Dolemite. New York rapper, Inga DeCarlo Fung Marchard, took on the name Foxy Brown during her rap career and the character Dolemite, played by Rudy Ray Moore, made a cameo appearance on Snoop Dogg's 1999 No Limit album. These characters and many others would inspire many other future Hip Hop songs and rappers.

The soundtracks of these movies were legendary. Soul music icons such as Bobby Womack, James Brown, Rose Royce, Roy Ayers, Herbie Hancock, and Willie Hutch provided the necessary grooves. Hip Hop djs would later sample all these artists and quite a few more from the movie genre. They laid down many a well-looped or chopped beat for talented lyricists to flow to and energized kids to dance to. Hip Hop was magical in that it introduced us to the music our parents partied to, sans the silky vocals, but frequently skillfully scratched.

It's ironic that Blaxploitation movies were among the bricks that served as part of the foundation of Hip Hop, while at the same time diluting the powerful Black progress made during the 1960's. The negative stereotypes featured in these films helped tear down the Black pride and healthy self-esteem we had built up during the Black Power movements. After Van Peeble's film in '71, the genre was co-opted by Europeans who fed us heaping mounds of chitterlings and hog maws through tacky, derogatory narratives and debasing imagery. Proud brothers and sisters soon gave way to poisonous personalities content to be addressed as niggas and bitches. Blaxploitation, or Black exploitation movies, as owned and created by Europeans, taught us to embrace the above-mentioned self-defeating terms as endearment. Hip hop eventually came to feel this pain too.

Mr. Gil Scott Heron was the "Grandfather of Hip Hop". Throughout the 70's in the years leading up to Hip Hop's actual birth, Gil Scott flowed rhythmically over soulful sounds and African drums. Heron's cadence and delivery were different than what most rappers came to offer as bars or verses. His songs were packed with social commentary, politics, and keen observations from the vantage of Black people in cities being shaped and impacted by environments within resource-deprived dense populations of us. Heron was spittin' knowledge, a main component of Hip Hop at its inception (he would later lament about the self-destructive elements that came to dominate Hip Hop in the 1990s). Nina Simone said it best, "You can't help it. An artist's duty, as far as I'm concerned, is to reflect the times." Gil Scott Heron fulfilled his duty as an artist masterfully. Many Hip Hop artists later followed suit.

Gil Scott-Heron performing in Bristol, England at the WOMAD festival, 1986
(Wilkipedia.com, 2020)

The paradigm shift in Hip Hop saw it transition from a potent and empowering force, a la Gil Scott, to heavy doses of self-destruction and Blaxploitation lyricism. Many of today's Hip Hop artists are no longer focused on Black elevation, the focus today is on getting paid while being a tool utilized to solidify the status quo. Zooming that picture out a bit, we can easily point to the same exploitation as we, as African people ascend corporate ladders, posture and pander as politicians, patrol and prosecute as law officers, certify and train as teachers in institutions of miseducation, and as we maneuver our way about Hollywood and sports arenas in entities and institutions we do not own, subject to being owned. It's not just our young rap artists being exploited today, it's the nature of existence for many of us, Black survival in a White world. The line between surviving and living is blurred; compensation is compromising and convoluting the picture.

CHAPTER 3
The Golden Age of Hip Hop

Many a rap aficionado will cite the late 80's to the mid 90's (1986-1996) as being the "Golden Age of Hip Hop". I call this span of time Hip Hop's transitional years. The Golden Age of Hip Hop featured innovative acts, a multitude of styles, some of Hip Hop's best lyricists, crisp production, and a good deal of balance. Hip Hop was knowledge and positivity, but it was also street sonnets and negative themes. The Golden Age was a good mix of the yin and the yang. Some of the more conscious artists were still present during this era, but the levees were breaking, making way for the gratuitous toxic imagery that would come to rule the space.

The Golden Age was rife with golden talent. Eric B & Rakim, De La Soul, Slick Rick, Big Daddy Kane, EPMD, Brand Nubian, A Tribe Called Quest, and KRS-ONE were among my favorites. Some acts promoted pure party fun like DJ Jazzy Jeff & The Fresh Prince. As mentioned, the streets had a voice during this period too. The Geto Boys, Ice-T, NWA, and 2 Live Crew held down the culture's raunchier aspects.

Chuck D of Public Enemy, Malmo, Sweden,1991. (DigitalJournal.com, Markos Papadatos, 2018)

It should not be overlooked that Hip Hop's gradual degradation coincided with its being co-opted by large, apathetic, European distribution companies. Hip Hop wasn't evolving as one would expect it to, being such a dynamic culture filled with so much creative and ingenious talent. It started as a powerful cultural tool but was gradually becoming something that devalued that culture. My peers and I can attest to a time when Hip Hop made it cool to learn about and embrace Black history and culture. Its transition saw it becoming a music form where values, morals, and principles took a back seat. Black artists were being paid well to purvey negative messages. Hip Hop was being gradually watered down and destroyed, controlled by entities and individuals who historically have made large fortunes exploiting Black people.

During the Golden Era, Hip Hop appeared confused, convoluted, and contorted. It featured a multitude of conflicting themes, but somehow that balance was maintained. Tupac Shakur was a Golden Age rapper whose career reflected the era's duality. Pac's mother, Afeni Shakur, was a Black Panther. His stepfather, Mutulu Shakur, is a currently incarcerated Black Liberation Army member, and his godfather, Geronimo Pratt (Jiga), was a Black Panther who was dealt the same wrongful incarceration card as Mutulu before his eventual release after serving 27 years in prison. Tupac's godmother is Assata Shakur, who was also a Black Liberation Army member, along with Mutulu. She is currently living as a protected political refugee in Cuba. Tupac's immediate influences growing up as a child were members of potent Black organizations charged with the emancipation of Black people from the chains of Western oppression. Afeni's, Mutulu's, Geronimo's, and Assata's impact on Tupac were evident. He possessed an awareness of America's social and political environment that many rap artists of the time did not, and he often rapped about these social and political realities in his music. Tupac made music that empowered Black women. *Dear Momma* and *Keep Ya Head Up* were two strong songs that immediately come to mind. As a young man, Tupac possessed the charisma and potential to become a solid Black leader had he been fortunate enough to be granted more than 25 years on this planet. His life was cut short by a bullet launched from the contrived conflict pitting Hip Hop's East Coast against its West Coast. He had millions of young men and women hanging from his words; the hustlers in the streets, the conscious community, and Black college students.

Tupac's messages of Black love later gave way to a

more acidic tone. Death Row Records gave us misogynistic, materialistic, and murderous Tupac. It was those murder-themed messages that helped bring about not only his own death, but the death of another rap legend, the Notorious BIG. The deaths of these two rap legends eventually led to the dissolution of the back and forth between New York and LA, but the tone of rap music continued on that downward spiral into the shallow abyss. Tupac's descent into the degrading and self-destructive mirrors Hip Hop's transition during those Golden Years. The vested Africans who created Hip Hop were losing the reigns to corporations who sought control of Hip Hop. That control was eventually manifested as a culture unrecognizable to its roots. The messages were becoming more negative and those who were taking ownership were making lots of money manipulating the artists to promote negativity. The Golden Age gave way to gangsterism.

CHAPTER 4
Gangster

In the late 1990's, the music industry decided it no longer had use for Hip Hop that empowered Black youth. The acts that got paid and promoted began to look and sound more like NWA. The industry, now totally under the control of individuals who looked nothing like the actual artists, decided that conscious Hip Hop would occupy a much smaller percentage of what was promoted and played. Public Enemy had reached its apex in 1990 and had remained consistent delivering potent messages with songs like *Shut Em Down*, *Fight the Power*, *Channel Zero*, and *Burn Hollywood Burn*. Chuck D and others were teaching. Black youth, I included, were listening and learning. Public Enemy had four albums that were either certified platinum or gold prior to being deprioritized. Why was it decided they would no longer be promoted? It was determined by rap's new owners that rap as a tool that took us to school would be moved to the basement, subjugated to the underground.

There is a particularly potent precedent that paralleled what was occurring in Hip Hop. During the 1960's, Black Nationalism, Black Power, and Black Pride were blossoming movements. X-Clan, Public Enemy, Brand Nubian, KRS-1 and similar acts fueled positive self-identity and self-esteem in Black kids during the 1980's and early 1990's. The Black Panthers, the Black Liberation Army, and the Nation of Islam instilled that same awareness in youth during the 1960's.

Black Power movements had their roots in early

independence movements in the Caribbean and on the African continent. At the turn of the 20th century, Marcus Garvey led the nationalist struggle from the wheel of his organization, the Universal Negro Improvement Association. He pushed to get Black people to understand the importance of Black Pride and autonomy. Garvey influenced activists of the 1960's such as Malcolm X, Kwame Ture, Huey Newton, Bobby Seale, Angela Davis, and Assata Shakur. They all were significant threats to uproot America's debilitating status quo.

A nation of awakened Black people is a threat to America's racist, classist, ways of being. America felt the urgent need to put Black people back to sleep. In the 1970s, Blaxploitation movies immediately followed a decade's worth of Black pride, self-esteem building, and Black love. These movies targeted Black audiences and effectively diluted and destroyed much of the self-esteem that had been cultivated during the 1960s. We enjoyed the movies without a full understanding of the propaganda being employed. These movies hosted Black heroes in the context of the most degrading images and narratives. After about a decade or so, the lives of Black people began to fully mimic what was depicted in these targeted media attacks. Powerful Black movements gave way to debasing and debilitating Black movies. Mass media was employed as a weapon against Black culture.

The U.S. government, much like the German Nazi government during WWII, has always been clear on the power mass media possesses. They've always understood its ability to influence the population; to affect people's thinking. In 1967, amidst Black Nationalist movements and increasing Black rioting in America, a group was convened by President Lyndon B. Johnson to investigate the causes of the 1967 race riots and to provide recommendations for the future. The race riots were a proud Black people's natural reaction to decades worth of crippling oppression. Blacks were rioting in communities all over the United States. The group Johnson pieced together was known as the Kerner Commission, named after its chairmen, Governor Otto Kerner Jr. of Illinois. The commission concluded that the causes of Black rebellion were the widening economic gulf between Whites and Blacks. Blacks were, as a result of lop-sided policies and discrimination, exponentially more impoverished and unemployed than Whites. The report also cited federal housing initiatives that created Black ghettos that lacked resources and adequate social programs. Hostile and predatory policing were also to blame. Even though President Johnson established the committee, he opted to ignore the solutions suggested by the commission to answer the problems that were plaguing Black people in America. These problems were rooted in institutionalized racism. Instead, Johnson signed into law the Civil Rights and Voting Rights Acts. These laws granted Black people more access to voting and additional access through integration but did nothing to curb systemic racism or the manifestations of systemic racism.

Wise Intelligent of Poor Righteous Teachers summarizes the findings of the Kerner Commission: (paraphrased)

".. Blacks were tired of the system and being oppressed by it, so young Blacks began to riot and burn things. . the commission found that the riots were mostly perpetrated by young Blacks motivated by high self-esteem and enhanced racial pride. . the majority of the rioters were high school dropouts who had a higher political orientation than their peers who remained in school. . the youth saw the system as their enemy so they attacked it. . fast forward to 1992, the #1 song on the radio is Public Enemy's *Fight the Power*. .in that same year, Rodney king gets beaten by L.A. Police before the world and the youth rebelled against the system as a result. . these youth in 1992 were primed by positive Hip Hop like Public Enemy, X-Clan, Poor Righteous Teachers, and Brand Nubian who helped cultivate Black youth with messages of pride, unity, independence, and empowerment. .in 1967, the Kerner Commission discovered that it was racial pride fueling the riots, so in 1970-71 they began killing the pride the Black youth had by flooding the theatres with Blaxploitation movies such as *The Legend of Nigger Charley*. .these movies brought down the racial pride and self-esteem of Black people. . during the 1980's, groups like P.E. brought back the racial pride and instilled it into the youth. . Black youth wanted to hear speeches from Dr. Josef Ben-Jochannan and Minister Farrakhan as opposed to spending time and money at strip clubs. . kids were motivated towards positivity. . . fast forward to 2006. .Sean Bell is shot 50 times by the N.Y. Police and no one does anything. . the #1 Hip Hop song on the radio in 2006 was *Like a Lollipop*. ." – *Lollipop* is a rap song by Lil Wayne that makes frequent references to sex/oral sex.

Our political orientation was disoriented and destroyed.

The same way the Blaxploitation Era arrested Black progression after the Black Power movements, Gangster rap was employed to try to erase any semblance of awakened Black youth during the Hip Hop era. As European/Jewish record industry executives strategically began to shift Hip Hop from a teaching tool to a destructive weapon, they gradually eliminated positive acts from Hip Hop's mainstream and began to showcase the poisonous. Gangster Rap was raised into prominence and heavily promoted. Those who rapped about Black genocide and misogyny got paid, while conscious artists were cast aside.

There were gangster artists who tried to right the ship and balance out the negativity in their music with messages of empowering truth. Young Buck attempted to release a song on an album that focused on the terrorism committed by police in America, but it was rejected by Jimmy Iovine of Interscope records who insisted that the song may create an unsafe environment for the police. What's crazy is the rest of the album, which frequently promoted killing Black men, was never mentioned as potentially endangering the lives of Black men. Blue lives matter more than Black ones to Mr. Iovine.

The historically misogynistic Too-Short mentioned in more than one interview that he wanted to abandon the disrespectful, misogynistic lyrics he'd been known for throughout his career. He wanted to try to do a conscious album but was soundly rejected by those who determine what gets promoted by Black rap artists. Too Short is one among a few who had decided to change course and do something positive musically but were refused. Essentially, conscious messages are censored, while abject ignorance is promoted. Mainstream artists who elect to produce albums with positive intent are discouraged from doing so and are urged to produce songs that feature the negative stereotypes, misogyny, disrespect, degradation, dehumanization, desensitization, and criminalization. Toxic music helps fuel the mass incarcerations of Black people in this country and in worse cases, our elimination. The bombardment of the minds of the youth with music that inspires them to be "less than" plays a role in the onset of a multitude of negative behaviors. It doesn't help that the perceptions a lot of police officers have of Black children are partially shaped by how Black children are portrayed in mainstream media, often as murderous maniacs. It's easier to justify mistreating and killing human beings who aren't perceived as being quite human by their apathetic antagonists.

It appears that large major record companies began to employ the use of propaganda through Hip Hop music as a means of subjugation. The same sort of propaganda was employed against the Jews by the Nazis in the years leading up to WWII. The Nazis sought to prime the Jews for extermination by depicting them, through Nazi-owned media, as subhuman and unworthy of existence. Negative depictions of the Jews opened the door for Hitler's Final Solution, the genocide of Jewish people. We'll discuss this scenario in detail later. Today, Hip Hop is largely owned by Jews who are employing the same use of propaganda which lends to the incarceration and elimination of Black people. While the main motive is always money, there is a historical relationship between Blacks and Jews that we will visit later that sheds light on the nature of that dynamic. As evidenced by the Jewish Holocaust, once you've dehumanized people through the use of negative propaganda campaigns (gangster rap, television and movies featuring negative stereotypes, unbalanced and distorted nightly news stories, inaccurate and eschewed history, etc.), it allows the dehumanized to be treated as disposable without there being any resistance from those witnessing it. Often, the propaganda is so potent that it compels the witnesses who look like the victims to join in that chorus of blaming the victims for being victims. This totally absolves the actual antagonists. We have seen how this works. Malcolm X warned us.

Enter NWA

In 1986, the rap group, Niggaz Wit Attitudes (N.W.A.), was formed. They were among the first, if not the first, mainstreamed gangster rap group. Their birth corresponded with the mainstream death of Public Enemy. Seemingly, P.E. had to die in order for N.W.A. to be born, and Hip Hop, as we knew it, died as well. Hip Hop, as an anti-Black weapon, was born. Life and death cannot occupy the same space. The version of Hip Hop promoted by its new European/Jewish owners has served as a sleeping gas bomb rendering black youth unconscious. Black youth were already facing the oppressive conditions and circumstances that come in concert with the racist policies and politics that hinder the healthy development of Black youth in America. Further media marginalization through gangster rap added to that already thick, toxic gumbo of the destructive. Far too many Black kids were already dealing with impotent schools, unstable households, poverty, unemployment, gang violence, drug and alcohol addiction, malnutrition, substandard healthcare, inadequate mental health care, oppressive policing, and mass incarceration. In addition to the aforementioned, Western society has always viewed Black people in general as having no real value. Degrading Hip Hop, under the guise of entertainment, is just another covert weapon of status quo maintenance.

I was 16 years old when NWA was first released. I lost my

mind (not realizing the literal sense applied). For my peers and I, it was Hip Hop. NWA was dope beats and lyrics to match. I ran to the store to cop it as soon as I got a taste. I was hooked. NWA was a breath of fresh air that hosted our rebellious spirits and a huge middle finger to a society that we were quickly learning didn't care about us. I was definitely a fan. I was too young and impressionable to notice the soul gradually being sucked out of Hip Hop by the music industry that had coopted it. As a teenager, I lacked the necessary frame of reference to gauge the impact of an NWA. I fully embraced and enjoyed the profound levels of ignorance and misogyny the music industry promoted through groups like NWA.

Rap with "gangsterish" content had cracked the door open eons ago but had still been relegated to the basement. We had to go underground to get it, fumbling through the music store record shelves to find it. N.W.A. kicked down that basement door and left it open for the emergence of a slew of dozens of other similar acts. N.W.A. was in many ways, the beginning of what exist today as Hip Hop. The "trap" was set.

Eventually, Gangster Rap ruled the Hip Hop landscape. The vibe that featured the murders of Black men and the frequent disrespect of Black women spread to the East Coast and then Down South. It got dirtier. N.W.A.'s initial fandom came from Black kids who loved Hip Hop, but eventually that core audience changed. Suburban White kids became (75%) of Hip Hop's consumers. (SoundData, 1994) As has always been the case, White kids wanted to know what life in "the hood" was like without actually falling victim to it. N.W.A. allowed them a virtual window into what they came to romanticize as Black reality. Meanwhile, N.W.A was touring and selling out seats at concert venues. Their concerts were largely populated by curious Caucasians and federal agents, agents whose feathers were ruffled by songs like *Fuck the Police*. Black youth were internalizing NWA's negative messages and the attached imagery and rededicating themselves to treating one another like the bitches and niggas of the Blaxploitation Era. White kids were internalizing these images and messages as well and growing into adults who saw Black youth as niggas, bitches, and thugs. Many of those young White NWA fans grew up to be White police officers who treat all Black people like bitches, niggers, and thugs. Reality is, that racist mindset had long ago been quite embedded. America is saturated with it. What better way to reinforce America's racist status quo than with repeated generations of negative propaganda serving to further cement how Black people are viewed in this country and around the globe. Where conscious Hip Hop was inspiring, uplifting, and teaching, Gangster Rap was doing exactly what Blaxploitation movies did to us in the 70's, dousing those freedom flames with codeine and coonery. Hip Hop was well beyond our control.

NWA's initial members consisted of Eric Wright (Eazy E), Andre Young (Dr. Dre), and O'Shea Jackson (Ice Cube). Eazy and Dre were from Compton, and Cube was from South Central. Eazy founded the group with profits from the drug hustle and brought Dre and Cube into the fold. Dre had been a member of the World Class Wreckin' Crew and was already a fairly accomplished DJ with a great ear for music. Ice Cube was an accomplished local lyricist when he joined NWA.

Consistent with many of Hip Hop's other super groups, a well-connected Jew put NWA on. Jerry Heller, an already established record industry head, introduced himself to NWA and eventually gave them access to fame and fortune. Unfortunately, the fortune part came in very small increments and much later for both Dre and Cube who eventually left NWA citing impropriety on the part of Heller. They both beefed with Eazy who they felt allowed Jerry Heller to wield too much influence over the group. They also accused both Eazy and Heller of cuffing a lot of their money. Cube had already written for two albums that sold a total of 5 million copies but wasn't paid enough to move out of his mother's home. Dre had already produced on albums for several acts under his contract but had barely made six figures, if that. Eazy E made substantially more than his band mates prior to his premature death at the age of 30. Prior to his death, Cube had left the group and experienced success with a string of conscious/semi-conscious albums. Dre later followed suit. Dre partnered with Suge Knight to produce his own albums and albums for Snoop Dogg and Tupac. While Dr. Dre's beats were otherworldly, the content on most of the albums he produced was very terrestrial; carnal. Black women were served up as the objectified and Black men saw no value in other Black men beyond seeing one another as bullet bait. Sonic self-destruction was now en vogue.

A Historical & Sociological Perspective

Eric Wright (Eazy E) & Jerry Heller, NWA's manager. (Factmag.com, 2020)

At the end of the day, I do not totally fault Black kids from marginal economic backgrounds for accepting stacks of cash from record executives to promote misogyny and violence. Throughout the history of Blacks in America, the prevailing set-up has been the Black pawn who has been paid handsomely by rich Whites to elevate him or herself at the expense of the Black collective. This dynamic isn't new. That exploitation has always been a component of both racism and capitalism. I'm no more surprised at young Black men and women signing contracts to promote Black self-destruction than I am young Black men and women getting paid to distribute drug death throughout Black communities. Poverty breeds compromise. As a collective, we are a compromised community. Our culture, as a whole, is compromised. With that compromise comes unhealthy, convoluted behaviors justified as survival. Had my peers and I been presented with some of these same opportunities as artistic youngsters, it's quite possible we could have been one of these groups being used as puppets to promote our collective self-degradation. We wanted the shiny, expensive material goods we saw promoted on MTV (Music Television) and BET (Black Entertainment Television) but we lacked the means to acquire them.

Stable households and present, capable, and interested parents make a difference. Among the first things this government did upon our involuntary arrival to America as property in the 16th century was fragment and destabilize Black families. Those efforts have continued to the present with the advent of welfare policies, the influx of drugs and guns into Black communities, collective disenfranchisement, unemployment, mass criminalization and mass incarceration. A lot of Black youth come from homes that have been functionally destabilized. Black communities mirror this very functional dysfunction. It's world's bigger than just placing the blame on Black kids or their parents. They both qualify as low hanging fruit. Missing the forest for the trees.

Not many of my generation or any successive generation missed out on opportunities to have our subconsciouses polluted with propaganda posing as music. In my more impressionable years, I was a huge fan of Mobb Deep. For me, Mobb had NWA faded, but the subject matter of the songs was essentially the same. They rapped about killing other Black men with some manic misogyny mixed in for good measure. We all embraced what was presented as entertainment to us; we all enjoyed it. We're living the manifestations of what was fed to us. We never demanded it, but overnight it became the bulk of what was supplied.

We have to begin to do three things. We have to target the beast, the industry, which profits mightily targeting Black people with debilitating images of ourselves. We have to educate and inform our children about the nature of the music industry and the economic system, capitalism, so they don't allow themselves to be played as weapons against us. Lastly, we have to begin to hold those artists accountable who make that conscious decision to allow themselves to be employed as poisonous propaganda puppets. Mind you, it isn't just the kids who are being played, many of our adults are employed in the same capacity. It isn't just the entertainment industry that sees Blacks positioned as ploys against the Black collective. We should all take a closer look at the nature of our own employment by others. Are we operating in the interests of or against the interests of the Black race?

At present, it is only Black people who are being targeted with our own self-destruction over every medium in the mainstream. It's affecting our psychological well-being. NWA were obvious tools and their fame rests upon the fact that they were a major factor in the partial disappearance of groups like Public Enemy. I partied to NWA as an impressionable child but as a conscious adult, I fully understand what they were, properly contextualized. I'm still awaiting that Public Enemy biopic from Hollywood. I won't hold my breath though.

In defense of the culture I love dearly, Hip Hop didn't give birth to media-promoted gangsterism, murder, and misogyny. America is saturated with it. America was occupied, stolen, founded, facilitated, and funded by gangsterism, plenty murder and misogyny. As a corollary, its politics, policies, and its media are infused with these despotic toxins. Broadening our perspective, America's domestic and foreign policy agendas encompass the same. Gangster rap is simply the manifestation of the marginalized mimicking the dominant culture. America is the biggest gangster on the planet earth. Hollywood does a magnificent job of glorifying America's militaristic, maniacal mannerisms, rendering them palatable to a patriotic proletariat. In many regards, gangster rap is rife with class struggle; the have-nots, through desperate means, seeking to come from under the boots of those who have. Gangster rap can't help but be riddled with misogyny. Women have always been oppressed in America. That objectification can't help but to be parlayed into the music of a subculture now owned by some of the greatest purveyors of the mistreatment of women. Reality is, those in power have always promoted what amounts to a sick society. They've conquered under its banner. As a race of subjugated and oppressed people, we cannot afford to imitate America. We must rediscover our culture and ourselves as weaponry to fight this war being waged against us. We've got to own our own mediums; we've got to own what gets messaged to our children.

CHAPTER 5
Identity Crisis

"When a man's history is written by his master's religion or economic philosophy, such history is always distorted to suit the master-slave relationship, which is the only possible result from such an enforced union. Such paternalism does not have to be vindictive. The mere fact of the relationship's existence forces one to feel, in fact, superior to the other, and if the history of such a union is of very long duration, many of the captured begin to accept their status of inferiority. They then allow themselves to be renamed accordingly. With their new NAME, a new psychology naturally develops, and with the new mind, a new docility"

- Dr. Yosef Ben-Jochannon -

I've observed for awhile that in the majority of the conversations I have with peers, the word "nigga" is employed. I hear it in the schools I work in and am forced to redirect it from students of every hue; blacks, browns, and whites. I stopped trying to address it with my peers with the realization that it's embedded into our language. We use the word unconsciously. It's about as involuntary as blinking or breathing. Every African male has become a nigga as looked upon by those within his circle. The use of the word was first targeted at Black people fueled by the hatred of racist Whites. That hate was tangible; it was felt. It's been internalized. The frequent use of the word as endearment from one Black man to another evidences a subtle, subconscious self-hatred we have yet to acknowledge and address adequately as a collective.

By definition, a person who is afflicted with self-hatred feels inadequate in some way. It is a feeling that is deeply ingrained and therefore resistant to persuasion or evidence. It's rare that you can convince someone that they hate themselves, especially when that person presents them self as having high self-esteem or confidence. Again, self-hate is subtle, but its manifestations are very tangible. We see the manifestations in the difficulty we have uniting behind a common cause that lends to collective progression. Self-hatred took centuries to install into the psyches of African people. Under the most psychologically debilitating conditions we became afflicted and it's been passed down from one generation to the next. We'd been conquered, kidnapped, and placed in a foreign land that sees us disconnected from our true selves. We have yet to adjust. One of the manifestations of that maladjustment is our proclivity towards adorning one another with the nigga label.

Largely as the result of Black Pride movements, we saw one another as soul siblings, brothers and sisters. Conscious Hip Hop had the same positive effect. We even looked upon each other as royalty, kings and queens. The Blaxploitation movie era socialized us into a subconscious sunken place. Nigga became a term of endearment. With the contrived advent of gangster rap a decade or so later, we became niggas at the same clip. This term of endearment was perpetuated and promoted through the music. As the music changed, so did the messages. Our collective behaviors, words, and the way we relate to one another changed as well. Our morals, ethics, and values changed. Our culture changed. Neither Blaxploitation nor gangster rap presented the first instances where we directed toxic terms at one another. To be called a Negro was an insult for decades before any media infected us. We've always had colorful ways to degrade one another. We've been doing the dozens for a pretty long time. Hip

Hop, at its inception, wasn't all rainbows, sunny skies, and fairy dust in regard to language, but when did the negative and toxic become the majority of what's heard, "mainstreamed" and normalized?

The word nigger is among the most despicable words in the English language. Its roots are found in the use of the word "negro" by the Portuguese to identify the African people they encountered on the continent as they began to invade in the late 15th century. In Portuguese and Spanish, the word negro means black. It began as a loose description of the beautiful Black people they encountered. As mercantilism, capitalism, and the Middle Passage kicked in, that description began to be conveyed as an insult. The darker colors of Africa's indigenous came to represent humans to be devalued, exploited, and enslaved. Eventually, English enslavers adopted the word and it morphed into the word nigger. The word had the effect of dehumanizing an entire race of people and casting them as beasts or animals unworthy of the rights or dignities afforded other human beings.

The word came to define all African people in America. During Reconstruction, the Black Codes Era, the Jim Crow South, and on up through the Civil Rights Era, the word "nigger" continued to be used by racist White people as a term of domination and ownership over African people. The Klu Klux Klan and other mobs of frothing at the mouth racist degenerates employed the word as they burned Black homes, businesses, churches, and Black bodies. Niggers became those beaten on wooden posts and lynched in trees. The words "kill that nigga" served as the chorus. Today, the words "kill that nigga" serve as the chorus. Every other song on European-owned urban radio stations is a dedication to Black fratricide with dead "niggas" gunned down all over rap tracks.

Naturally, the word "nigga" wasn't a fashionable term employed by us during our earlier residency here in America, but it remained part of our enemy's vocabulary. The word has existed since America's beginning as part of America's truth. Today, most racists use the protection of the internet and keyboards to direct the weaponized term at Black people. At present, many Black people direct the word nigga at one another as an unhealthy substitute for "brotha" or "sista". It saturates most of our mainstream music. Many of our rappers do not feel like we can complete a bar in a song unless we use it. Today, it's popular to promote this subtle self-hatred throughout our music. The music industry's owners love it.

CHAPTER 6
The Birth of a Nation

In 1915, millions of Americans saw the first full-length motion picture projected on to an American big screen. It seems befitting, with America's history, that this country's first big screen production would be utilized to further dehumanize and disrespect its most volatile and discriminated against citizens. The name of the movie was *Birth of a Nation*. This movie marked a major resurgence of the dehumanization of Black people through mass media. Earlier minstrel shows, print media, and word of mouth had for centuries been accomplishing these destructive aims, but nowhere near as impactfully and effectively as a motion picture. *Birth of a Nation* was a silent black and white movie directed and co-produced by D.W. Griffith. It's been touted as an artistic and innovative marvel along with earning recognition as among the most racist movies ever made. Black men, played by White men, were portrayed as brutal savages who lusted after White women. Black men were shown as members of Congress whose main aspiration in life was to secure the right to marry White women. With faces painted black, White men depicted Black men who, with bare feet kicked up, frolicked in Congress conducting the business of disenfranchising White people while eating chicken and drinking whiskey. The movie was one racist stereotype or trope after another, quite the spectacle. Hollywood hasn't missed a beat since the production of this poisonous propaganda piece, and both socially and psychologically, Blacks in America have paid the price for these damning portrayals.

Birth of a Nation was the resurgence of the minstrel show. Minstrel shows were shows performed by White men in front of White audiences where the performers painted their faces Black to depict Black men. Every single stereotype used to defame Black people during the early part of the 20th century is still pervasive in mass media today. Fried chicken eating, lazy, drunk, sex-driven, dim-witted, subservient, and overly fearful docile men were some of the main stereotypes being pushed on to the psyches of moviegoers. Around this time, Blacks couldn't get roles acting so Whites seized the opportunities and got paid well pretending to be those they despised.

From the motion picture, Birth of a Nation. Directed by D.W. Griffith, 1915.

Eventually, Blacks were allowed to land roles as actors and actresses on stages and on big screens. However, the writers, producers, and directors of these movies were always White/Jewish, and as a result, Blacks were forced to play roles where they reinforced the same stereotypes featured in the minstrel shows. America's racism saturates Hollywood so Black performers were paid far less than White face-painters. A handful of Black actors/actresses managed to make a decent living basically working as

Black minstrels. Lincoln Perry was the first such Black actor. He played the lazy, barely audible, clumsy idiot, Stepin Fetchit. He started his career on big screens in 1927 and went on to become a very rich man portraying Black men as having little or no value. Off-screen, Lincoln Perry was said to be a pretty intelligent and insightful human being. However, the unfortunate reality is that he was willing to compromise himself and the Black collective for fame and fortune. Throughout our history in America's entertainment industry, this has been our lot. In order to make it big, we've had to belittle ourselves. It's the 21st century, and in many regards, we're still compromising ourselves to gain access to Hollywood and other media platforms. Ownership of our mediums yields ownership of ourselves. We have to keep moving towards that shift.

Like the present, there were Black people who angrily protested the Stepin Fetchit character, understanding the psychological damage done by his depictions. Today, most of these sorts of protests tend to fall on deaf ears. Participation is thin as a good many of us are only interested in the entertainment aspects of what we consume in mass media. We don't necessarily feel the need to understand the propaganda aspects of what we allow ourselves to be entertained by. Tyler Perry set a precedent and created a template for Black success in the movie industry. Producing what promotes the status quo and growing prosperous. It didn't start with rap.

Decades after Stepin Fetchit, Black TV viewers were introduced to the show, 'Good Times', which featured actor Jimmy Walker. Jimmy Walker played the character J.J. Evans who was every bit the minstrel clown that Stepin Fetchit was, albeit very slightly more dignified. After some years, the show's White writers decided they wanted the court jester of a character, J.J., to be the focal piece of the show. Two of the other main characters on the show, John Amos and Esther Rolle, who played his very dignified parents, both protested the proposed change. They didn't want to be associated with any minstrel-like roles or performances. There have always been proud Blacks, including proud Black entertainers, who understood the damage done through the continued promotion of negative Black stereotypes. Unfortunately, there aren't ever enough organizing and committed to forcing those much-needed changes. John Amos was eventually written off the show and Esther Rolle left the show for a while only to return later. Again, rappers weren't the first to face these dilemmas of pride, principles, and the need to get paid. That snowball hasn't stopped rolling downhill. It is a gigantic mess today.

Top left: *Tom & Jerry* cartoon, William Hanna & Joseph Barbera, 1946-1954. **Top right**: *Nigga Charley, Martin Goldman,* 1972. **Bottom left**: Lincoln Perry as the subservient "Stepin Fetchit", 1927-1939. **Bottom right**: *Menace II Society,* Larenz Tate as "O-Dog". Directed by Allen and Albert Hughes, 1993. **Center**: *Heckle & Jeckle* cartoon. Created by Paul Terry, mid-20th century.

CHAPTER 7
Blaxploitation

Destructive and debasing propaganda that serves as entertainment for a targeted audience is analogous to the Trojan horse scenario. In ancient Greek mythology, a Trojan horse was a hollowed out wooden statue of a horse that the Greeks used in the Trojan War to enter the city of Troy. The Greek soldiers set the large statue just outside of the city of Troy. The Greek soldiers would then conceal themselves inside of the hollowed out wooden statue. Once the Trojans rolled the gift inside of their city, the Greeks would leap out surprising them, the gift quickly becoming a violent curse.

Trojan Horse

In many regards, the Blaxploitation movies of the 1970's were a Trojan horse. The Black mind was the city of Troy. Blaxploitation movies featured all or mostly Black casts. They came out at a time when Hollywood was struggling financially, but what better way to recoup those losses than on the backs of Blacks hungry to be represented in Hollywood, Black actors and actresses hungry for work in their crafts. The movies were rife with the most rancid themes White/Jewish movie executives could conjure up: misogyny, self-hatred, materialism, subservience, alcoholism, drug use, and drug dealing. Blaxploitation movies were presented to Blacks as gifts to be enjoyed. We were happy to have Blacks in movies and working in Hollywood. We flocked to the theatres to watch our new favorite heroes and heroines. We were thoroughly entertained. Black actors and actresses accepted many roles that painted us as every sort of devalued human being. In general, these rancid stereotypes were hidden within stories that presented the Black man or woman as a 'hood hero fighting against "the man".

The word nigger went into gratuitous use during the Blaxploitation era largely due to the titles like *The Legend of Nigga Charley*, *Run Nigga Run*, and *Boss Nigga*. These titles were overt disrespect. We accepted these titles for years and embraced the movies as entertainment to be enjoyed. We couldn't even mention the title of a Blaxploitation movie without having to utter our own defamation. We didn't realize it then, but what we were consuming as entertainment was making us sick. In actuality, it was propaganda rife with poisonous messaging and imagery. Our subconscious ingested and digested what was being fed to us from Hollywood studios owned and operated by Jews/Europeans. What was manifested was us seeing ourselves in what was presented to us on those big screens. The fictitious niggas became "real" ones. The sting of racism the word is innate with became a title we embraced as something to be great with.

A Historical & Sociological Perspective

Boss Nigga, directed by Jack Arnold, 1974.

One of the unfortunate facts about Blaxploitation movies was that Blacks didn't own them. We got to participate, play our parts, and get paid. We rarely took part in the production or writing of these movies. Blaxploitation flicks were largely the interpretations of Black culture as dictated by European/Jewish movie industry executives. The biggest exception would be Mario Van Peeble's and his film, *Sweet Sweetback's Baadasssss Song*. Although full of the negative imagery that helped launch the Blaxploitation era, Van Peeble's film featured a narrative that saw a brother rise above negative environmental elements, a racist system, and actually fight "the man" and win. Hollywood had a problem with the winning part of Van Peeble's script and refused to fund Mr. Van Peeble's effort. Despite their efforts to kill it, his film was a huge success, garnering him lots of popularity and cash.

Like many of the movies of the era, Sweetback hosted a soulful soundtrack that put some of the best Black music and Black musicians on display. Some of the best music of the 70's decade was featured in these movies helping to define the time period. Artists such as Bobby Womack, Dennis Coffey & Luchi De Jesus, James Brown, Norman Whitfield, Roy Ayers, Herbie Hancock, Willie Hutch, Curtis Mayfield, The Dells, and Marvin Gaye graced the sonic backdrops of these movies. Much of the music of the era featured a very distinct soulful and jazzy vibe. Juxtaposed with the messages promoted during Blaxploitation movies, the music was definitely the highlight.

The Blaxploitation era had a profound impact on Hip Hop culture. The pimp persona was one later adopted by artists like Too Short, Snoop Dogg, and Ice-T. Films such as *The Mack* and *Superfly* served as obvious influences. More contemporary artists like 50 Cent named one his more popular singles *P.I.M.P.* Naturally, the accompanying videos to some of these artists' songs featured luxury cars and scantily clad women. Misogyny and materialism eventually became consistent themes within the Hip-Hop genre.

Very functionally, these movies were redefining Black people and Black culture. The 1960's had seen us rising off of our backs and raising our fists to fight the power and reclaim our racial pride. The Blaxploitation era saw to it that any pride we had amassed during the 60's was decimated and replaced by our acceptance and ownership of the most belittling stereotypes and depictions. During this time, many of us came to see the words nigga and brother as synonymous. Misogyny against Black women also gained more fuel during this period.

Toward the end of the 70's, Black people began to awaken to the reality of what Blaxploitation movies represented. We began to see these productions as our own cinematic self-destruction. We began to defy and protest the negative imagery and portrayals promoted through Blaxploitation films. With evaporating support from us and pressure from Black advocacy groups, including the NAACP, the genre eventually disappeared. These movies eventually resurfaced decades later as cult favorites on different mediums, largely fueled by frequent Hip Hop mentions. The Blaxploitation Era, again, evidenced the urgent need for us to own our own media platforms.

CHAPTER 8
Context Matters

Propaganda naturally affects us beyond the realm of hip hop in ways that shape our self-image. Words are weaponized in a way that, over time, produce the desired mindset or frame of reference. This chapter is about one of the most subtle, yet powerful ways our thinking is manipulated. As Black people, we are all subjected to it with regularity.

From the time we first enter school as the young and impressionable, the normalization of our psychosis begins. Initially, we're too young to realize it, and as we age, the socialization process prepares us to deny it. Our interpretation of the world and ourselves is filtered through a colander that strains away any remnants of our ability to see ourselves through our own eyes, from our own vantage. Everything we observe and process is in the context of our centuries long captivity. DuBois called it "double-consciousness theory". In his book, *Souls of Black Folk,* DuBois "describes the sensation of feeling as though your identity is divided into several parts, making it difficult or impossible to have one unified identity." In other words, as a result of our oppression here, we devolve a self that is acutely aware and concerned about how we are viewed by Europeans and others in America. This often comes at the expense of our own self-identity. After a while, we subconsciously internalize our subjugated position and are unable to view ourselves as the fully capable Africans we are and have always been. We begin to lowball our own potential.

Jesse Owens in Berlin, Germany. 1936 Olympics.

Everything about our Eurocentric educations and the multiple forms of European-owned media we are exposed to throughout life in America shapes us. If we are not actively fighting to maintain our self-esteem, we are involuntarily surrendering it, and succumbing to self-imposed servility. The war for our minds is real. Among the most subtle yet potent ways in which our sense of self is chipped away is through the following ubiquitous statement:

"_____ was the first Black person to _____."

Thousands of teachers, especially History teachers, repeat this phrase every day in schools all across America. Black, Brown, and White teachers see this phrase as instilling racial pride in young Black children. They believe it evidences the multitude of achievements by Africans despite the uphill struggles. Actually, what the statement suggests is that Europeans are the bar setters, la primavera, the first to accomplish all there is to accomplish in this world. It suggests that Black people can only hope, at best, to be second behind the perpetual pioneers. Ask yourself when the last time was you heard the phrase, "_____ was the first White person to _____." I've honestly never heard it and I'm certain most of us can say the same. Hearing the former phrase hundreds of times throughout our lives very incrementally prepares us psychologically to accept second tier citizenship. We begin to speak of ourselves and our existence solely within the context and confines of our captivity here. We begin to subconsciously neglect the fact that African people have existed for thousands of years prior to being captured and transported across the Atlantic to America's shores. We had a glorious history before there was a European to speak of. In the context of a whole history, we were first to accomplish quite a bit. This is information that too many American educators neglect to impart, largely due to its functional omittance from most curricula. Words can be used to uplift, and they can be used as well to subjugate subconsciously. That second place we're socialized to embrace is synonymous with second class citizenship synchronized through systemic subjugation. Media we consume in the form of music and weaponized school curricula both serve to hammer in our collective psychosis.

CHAPTER 9
The Science of Sound Waves

The making of music that serves to bring about certain desired behaviors goes beyond the simple manipulation of the words. The actual sound waves music creates are subject to purposeful manipulation. Our dispositions can be adjusted through subtle changes in these sound waves. The soundwaves influence us through the water our bodies are largely composed of. Our bodies are composed of approximately 60-65% water. The moon affects the earth's large bodies of water similarly. The levels of large bodies of water worldwide are raised and lowered by the gravitational pull of the moon. Tides come in and go out with the moon's gravitational influence. The emotional moods of human beings are often affected by the varying phases of the moon as a direct result of the large amount of water our bodies are composed of. Our moods fluctuate like the tides. Most plants contain proportionally more water than humans and other animals and experiments have shown that plants tend to thrive when music is introduced into their space. Our foliage can appreciate a funky tune.

Sound waves are patterns of disturbance caused by the movement of energy traveling through a medium such as air or water as it moves away from the original source of the sound such as a stereo speaker. Sound waves are measured in units of hertz (Hz). Hertz is the standard unit of measurement used for measuring audio frequency. Since frequency is measured in cycles per second, one hertz equals one cycle per second. The hertz, as a unit of measurement, was named for the scientist, Heinrich

Rudolph Hertz, who was the first to find proof of the existence of electromagnetic waves.

It's been theorized that by adjusting the sound waves or Hz of music, the moods or mindsets of people can be adjusted or manipulated, similar to the way music can stimulate plant growth. In regard to the sound waves produced by music, 432 Hz reportedly reflects a more natural wave pattern. At 432 Hz, the mind is said to be more in tune with nature, with right minded thinking being stimulated. The right mind of human beings houses the faculties that bring about creativity, artistry, and imagination in people. At 432Hz, people are reportedly more at peace, relaxed, and not easily agitated. The other setting at which musical sound waves have been scientifically observed is 440Hz. Music played at 440Hz is said to promote more left brain functioning. Left brain functioning includes rigidity, logic, being more realistic, scientific, mathematical, and more prone to agitation. The wave pattern, as reflected on water, of 432Hz is far more fluid, symmetrical, smoother, and cohesive than sound wave patterns at 440Hz which appear more asymmetrical, inharmonious, frayed, and disjointed. Both 432Hz and 440Hz sound wave patterns are displayed in water the following photograph.

A Historical & Sociological Perspective

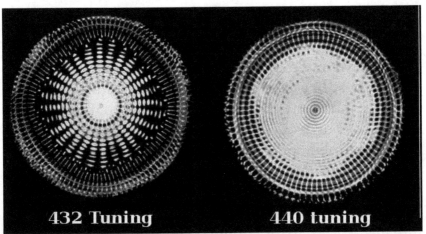

(Japanupdate.com, 2016)

In 1933, Adolph Hitler became the Chancellor of Germany and leader of the Nazis. He hired his friend, Joseph Goebbels, to serve as his Minister for Public Enlightenment and Propaganda. In this role, Goebbels's responsibilities included utilizing available mediums to portray Hitler in a positive light, dehumanizing and demonizing Jews, and regulating the content of all German media. Reportedly, Joseph Goebbels changed the Hz of music broadcasted in Germany from 432Hz to 440Hz to manipulate how the people of Germany felt and thought. This was said to be done in to render German citizens prisoners of a certain consciousness; hardworking, law-abiding, and obedient automatons.

Research has found that music played at 440Hz facilitates a mindset that makes people work harder, while curbing creativity and emotionalism. These would be traits desirable to a dictator and a regime seeking to create a nation of hard workers, scientists, mathematicians, and engineers. They could be easily controlled and devoid of critical thought or the inclination to create anything, a nation of drones.

In 1940, the United States introduced 440Hz as the universal standard and it was eventually accepted as the ISO (International Standards Organization) standard in 1953. I don't have the research to evidence the effect the 440Hz standard has had on the American population as a collective, but I know for certain that America has the highest number of incarcerated citizens in the world at around 2.3 million people. A number of other societal factors play roles in America's medieval incarceration rate. It can't be overlooked that well over half of America's inmates suffer from mental health issues. We also shouldn't gloss over the fact that a disproportionate number of America's inmates are Black and Latino. I would be curious to know the percentage of these Black and Latino inmates who have consumed and carried out the messages delivered through gangster rap finely tuned at 440Hz. Any correlation or connection is merely circumstantial without the benefit of exhaustive research, but we should always be clear on the fact that psychological warfare is an essential component of population control. When the minds of the masses are controlled by a few, those few benefit from certain desired behaviors within the populations they've conquered and subjugated. These manifested behaviors usually help pad the pockets of those who pull the strings in this society. In addition to the creation of worker bees, manipulated media helps produce criminals, along with people who possess the propensity to mindlessly consume material items. The aforementioned create profits. America is profit driven. Driving right over the backs of those it opts to exploit, Blacks and the poor.

CHAPTER 10

The Historical Relationship Between Blacks and Jews

"If we don't know ourselves, our culture, and our history, we will settle for being taken. I am not a religious person, but I do believe in heaven and hell. I believe them to be states of mind. Throughout life, we experience heaven and hell. The goal is to have as much control over our existence in either of these states of mind as possible. As a collective, we should be able to facilitate heaven for ourselves while not allowing anyone to impose hell on us. That is the very nature of being controlled. . whoever is in control of the hell in your life is your devil"
- John Henrik Clarke -

There is a historical relationship between African people and Jews that is rooted in such control. The following quote speaks to the nature of that control in the 17th and 18th centuries

". . .Jews also took an active part in the Dutch colonial slave trade; indeed, the bylaws of the Recife and Mauricia congregations (1648) included an imposta (Jewish tax) of five soldos (an Italian unit of money) for each Negro slave a Brazilian purchased from the West Indies Company. Slave auctions were postponed if they fell on a Jewish holiday. In Curacao, in the 17th century, as well as in the British colonies of Barbados and Jamaica in the 18th century, Jewish merchants played a major role in the slave trade. In fact, in all the American colonies, whether French (Martinique), British, or Dutch, Jewish merchants frequently dominated. . .this was no less true on the North American mainland, where during the 18th century, Jews participated in the 'triangular trade' that brought slaves from Africa to the West Indies and there exchanged them for molasses, which in turn was taken to New England and converted to rum for sale in Africa. Isaac Da Costa of Charleston in the 1750's, David Franks of Philadelphia in the 1760's, and Aaron Lopez of Newport in the late 1760's and early 1770's, dominated Jewish slave trading on the American continent."

- Rabbi Marc Lee Raphael -

If you know and understand the beginning of any relationship, you are better tooled to address the issues or problems that may arise during the course of it. The relationship between Blacks and Jews has historically been one that featured the economic exploitation of Blacks. This historical dynamic hasn't given way to a rosier picture in any regard. Jews owned us as slaves for centuries, and today, Blacks are owned in America's most profitable arenas, Hollywood, sports, and the music industry. The nature of that ownership reflects an unbalanced relationship that has perverted itself into a more palatable, yet equally oppressive reality. In many regards, our current hell is overseen by this arrangement.

A major component of any people's culture is the art its people create. Art comes in many different forms, but among the most impactful art forms is music. A culture's music traditionally encompasses its history, its norms, its morals, its achievements, its travails, and its ancestry. It reflects how the people within that culture relate to one another. Most importantly, a people's culture, when utilized as a tool, sustains and empowers the members of that culture. Unfortunately, Black culture in America is no longer owned by Black people. It is owned by others, generally corporations who do not have much regard for Black culture or the creativity borne of that culture. This results in Black culture being redefined by individuals who are focused on ways to exploit Black culture and Black artists to maximize profits. Black empowerment is not part of the equation. Those who control Black culture have bastardized it, convoluting its narratives, stories, and images in a way that distorts the perception of Black people. The way Blacks see themselves and relate to one another is directly influenced by this altered image of ourselves. In addition, the way other groups see Black people is also directly impacted. This redefining of who we are is pervasive and promoted across all mediums.

"To control a people, you must first control what they think about themselves and how they regard their history and culture. And when your conqueror makes you ashamed of your culture and your history, he needs no prison walls and no chains to hold you."

- John Henrik Clarke -

Dr. Clarke imparted to us years ago that we have no friends on this planet. Clive Davis (Jewish) appeared to be a friend to many Black recording artists. As a music industry executive at CBS, Arista, and Sony, he oversaw the careers of some of our most talented artists and maintained tight control of the messages in their music, their careers, and their personal lives. Whitney Houston (died of drug overdose), Michael Jackson (died of drug overdose), and Phyllis Hyman (drug overdose), were among the Black artists "managed" by Mr. Davis. The circumstances surrounding the deaths of these immensely talented individuals is worthy of suspicion, Davis also managed the careers of other incredibly talented songstresses, including Aretha Franklin and Angela Bofill. While Davis was known throughout the industry as a "star maker", he was also known as a manager who frequently took soulful Black music such as R & B and Jazz and rendered it Pop through the control and commercialization of the artists he managed as an industry power broker. Phyllis Hyman reportedly did not care for the sort of direction and manipulation Davis attempted to wield over her career and she wasn't shy about mentioning it in interviews. She attempted to gain control of her music during her career. Prince and Michael Jackson tried to gain ownership and control of their own art as well and suspiciously met the same fate as Ms. Hyman. As remarkable of a singer Whitney Houston was, when her cigarette smoking and drug use began to take its toll, Davis dropped her like a bad habit. Despite the amount of money Davis and the record company made from Whitney's talent, they had no tolerance for her bad habits. Black artists who battle for control of their own artistry tend to become incredibly disposable. The record companies seem to always wind up with total control of Black artists' work after the artists die. These greedy, exploitive companies are then free to profit mightily from those artists' songs posthumously without interference or conscience.

Sumner Redstone (Jewish) owns Viacom which owns Black Entertainment Television, MTV, and a lot of other media platforms. BET is known for its amazingly degenerate programming that features Black people filling every negative stereotype conceived. BET falsely attaches itself to Black culture while continuously airing the most egregious depictions of Black culture to the world. I have fond memories of watching BET's 106 & Park with hosts Free and AJ. That was back when BET was at least somewhat palatable, when it was still Black-owned. Nowadays, there's a guarantee that viewers will observe misogyny, mindless gossip, and violence on a consistent basis via shows such as "Love and Hip Hop", a ridiculous portrayal of Black womanhood. Imagine it, an entire TV channel dedicated to Black culture that features not an iota of Black empowerment. BET is commentary on the status of the Black collective; rich, robust, black coffee watered down with spoiled milk.

Left: Sumner Redstone (deceased), former owner of National Amusements/Viacom/BET. Right: Lyor Cohen. Former music executive with Def Jam and Warner, and current CEO of 300 Entertainment.

With more than thirty years of moving and shaking within the Hip-Hop community, a "tall Jew" somehow became the corporate face of a culture he had no part in creating. Lyor Cohen got his start as a manager of up and coming artists at Rush Records. He rose to become a top executive of one of the largest Black music companies since Motown, Def Jam. He oversaw dozens of Hip Hop artists' careers. Cohen has parlayed that initial position atop the Hip Hop world into a series of titles and positions that see him calling the shots for a multitude of artists. Mos Def touched on Cohen's influence in his song, *The Rape Over* where he mentions the tall Israeli running Hip Hop. Cohen is 6'5. The song mysteriously disappeared from Mos Def's album, The New Danger, with record executives claiming later that the issue was sample clearance. Under his various titles, Lyor has had the ability to manipulate Hip Hop culture by deciding where and to whom the money goes. He's had the power to make or break hip hop artists. Fairly recently, Cohen leveraged his resources and connections and helped start 300 Entertainment. Among the labels first signings were Fetty Wap and Young Thug. Both are artists who specialize in lyrics which degrade Black people.

Much like the National Football League, Hip Hop continues to consist of a majority of Black players who are owned by almost all Jewish men. That owner/owned dynamic hasn't changed at all over the course of almost four centuries. Its embedded in America's flag. We have accepted it; however, we operate from a position of power. We possess the creativity and talent. We have yet to wield that power in a fashion that sees Black people benefitting from Black gifts and talent.

Michael Jackson released a song, *They Don't Really Care About Us*, where he mentioned Jews in a context that was interpreted by Jewish media as being anti-Semetic. He was forced to re-issue the song with altered lyrics. On a Jay-Z album entitled *4:44*, there is a song entitled *The Story of OJ* where Jay Z makes a reference to the fact that Jews own a large amount of land in America. Just his mention of that easily researchable fact led the Jewish Anti-Defamation League (ADL) to come after him. What makes it more interesting is the fact that much of Jay Z's career was overseen by Lyor Cohen as a lead executive at Def Jam. Jay Z and dozens of other artists overseen by Cohen constantly refer to themselves and other Black people as niggas, bitches, and all sorts of other debasing terms. This self-destructive self-identification is always green-lighted. However, one cannot even mention the word Jew in rap music without drawing the ire of the Jewish community. This has everything to do with their ownership of most major media platforms. The word nigga is used freely and gratuitously throughout hip hop. Black women are referred to as bitches and many other derogatory names at a clip that suggest these misogynistic terms may morph into surnames for our sisters. What should be senseless to us makes perfect "cents" to them, dollars for them.

For Black voices to be heard in Hip Hop, they must meet the approval of Jewish executives. Corporate compensation keeps many a Black artist complicit. They are being forced to deliver debilitating messages to Black children through Jewish record executives who often demand they keep it toxic. That combination of fame and fortune are reserved for artists who deliver the debasing. For the longest, the elephant in the room has been the fact that Black culture is being controlled by Jewish men. I'm unable to imagine a scenario where Jews would allow Black men to control their culture. Picture a Black man at the helm of the Jewish Anti-Defamation League. We had the unfortunate precedent of the NAACP (National Association for the Advancement of Colored People), which serves as an instrument of Black advocacy, being founded, facilitated, and funded by predominantly Jewish people. We've been socialized to accept this sort of relationship and in many regards, the dynamic has manifested itself as ownership. Hip Hop culture used to serve as a vessel of Black advocacy, a Black empowerment tool. Much like Whitney before her tragic and unfortunate transition, we seem to have lost our voice.

CHAPTER 11
The Capitalist Con Game

America's schools tend to teach us only a very basic definition of capitalism. It's taught in a way where most Americans don't have a thorough understanding of the economic system, what it entails, or its profit driven manifestations. America's poor and exploited tend not to see capitalism as the major reason they are poor and exploited. We're taught that, as an economic system, capitalism is the fuel that powers the greatest country in the world. No mention is made of the inherent ominousness of a system that sees human beings stratified according to economic classes, a new age caste system. America's caste system leaves most people struggling to survive while a relative few consolidate the majority of America's wealth and resources. The poor are just human resources to be exploited by those at the top of the ladder. Their humanity doesn't matter. We are taught that we should be happy to reside in a free market society, but we never recognize our being slaves of the palatable variety. We have accepted our collective lot as cogs in capitalist machinery. We have been socialized to accept the notion of earning the right to eat, clothe one's self, and place a roof over one's head. We have embraced the idea of earning the right to live as if that right is not inherent from birth.

We are addicted to peonage. America's economic system features two forms of peonage, debt and wage. Debt peonage sees us accruing debt through devices such as college loans that lock us into the need to maintain steady employment, wage peonage. Once locked into this arrangement, most of us generally are never afforded the time, finances, or peace of mind to pursue endeavors that speak to our innate creativity. Overtime, we drift further and further away from our true selves as we settle into our roles within systemic servitude.

The best way to cultivate a population of citizens who embrace the idea of debt and wage peonage is to keep us distracted from the realization that we are indeed polished peons. Many of us go our entire lives without the realization that we possess the means to control our own means of existence as individuals and as a collective. It never becomes a collective goal. Capitalism requires that we buy into what the system offers as "earning" or "making" a living. Schools, through curricula and textbooks published by the world's major media conglomerates, mold us into roles and career paths that facilitate our acceptance of a life-limiting job or life as a human resource. If more schools offered students tangible opportunities for self-discovery, far fewer would accept assigned roles as employees. This is not to say that society has no room for employees. However, society has plenty of pie to share. Much of that pie is hoarded into the hands and mouths of a relative few.

(Jacqueline Martin, 2011)

A Historical & Sociological Perspective

(Yoddler.com/author unknown, 2020)

Today, we are witnessing capitalism cresting as institutions that were previously controlled, funded, and facilitated by the state are becoming privatized and for-profit. What better way to whittle down human beings than by subjecting them at young ages to curricula that is linearly focused on college preparation, in other words, job preparation. Most of our children are never introduced to musical instruments and quality music instructors within quality music programs.

"Musical opportunities are now concentrated in a small group of arts-focused schools, like the Celia Cruz Bronx High School of Music, which require auditions, while students at most high schools in the borough have little opportunity to play music."

(The New York Times, Natalie Proulx, 5/17/2018)

Most of our young students never see a quality vocational or apprentice program that tools them for a lifetime of self-sufficiency, armed with tangible skill sets, being able to subsist from their own innate gifts and talents. For the 2019-2020 school year, 62 public high schools in New York City. .

". .abruptly lost millions in crucial federal funding for vocational programs after the state changed the eligibility requirements for the schools to receive the money – forcing many schools to scramble, and some to make significant cutbacks. The financial cuts affect thousands of students – many of whom specifically chose high schools for their vocational offerings. ."

(New York Daily News, Michael Elsen-Rooney, 1/13/2020)

I can't tell you how many children I've met throughout my two decades as a secondary public school educator who were genius level artists with talents that will never be realized because they've been deemed either "pass" or "fail" by a standardized test. These tests were created to make certain only well-standardized students pass, the most well-polished cogs. The machine awaits them all.

The privatization of schools is manifested as the proliferation of charter schools. With charter schools, venture capitalists profit from "educating" poor students, while also tooling them for the profit driven institutions that are colleges and universities. These institutions of "higher learning" prep students for jobs they have been standardized to fill. There are a handful of media giants that happily provide the curricula and the textbooks that fuel our acceptance of America's debilitating economic system. Reality is, we've accepted America's governance and corrupt politics as well through the same socialization that sees us embracing peonage. In short, we are fertilized through a very narrow functional flow of information to blossom into "happy slaves". Many of us are the slaves our sister Harriet spoke of that couldn't be freed. We live entire lives captivated by capitalism's illusions as captives saddled with delusion. Freedom is relative.

Retail Pathology

A major component of capitalism is its ability to create consumers; to contrive consumption. Consumers drive the economy's gears. They drive gross domestic product gains. When people are buying, the economy is thriving. Every single class in America's caste system is baited with materialism. The accumulation of material goods is status for many. It is self-esteem for many. For some, it defines self-identity. It's scary how the health of many relationships in America are hinged on the accumulation of pennies. Fiat as a determinant of fidelity. The rich are targeted with bigger and better boats while the poor are saddled with the desire for the newest kicks. Boys grow into men who replace kicks with cars as a collection addiction. Ironically, we "grow" into adults who master the accumulation of liabilities. The hoarding of things is a Western disease.

If America is stricken with a disease of some sort, it tends to ravage the marginalized the most. Excessive consumption can be a bit more than a minor inconvenience for the rich, but they tend to have cushions and nets to break any financial falls they may be beset with. But for the poor, money mismanagement can be the difference between having a roof or no roof over one's head. It can be the difference between having a car and being forced to revisit fancy shoe collecting. The poor typically do not have much wriggle room to waste money. However, this reality does not prevent America from targeting the poor with the idea that they should mass consume. The minds of the marginalized consume these ideas through perfect product placement in television shows and movies. Strategically placed advertising around movies and television programming permeate the subconscious as well. Entertainment is a by-product, the purpose of corporate media is to constantly sell, sell, sell.

Corporate corrupted and coopted Hip Hop has not escaped becoming a vessel to create the manic materialistic. And through corporate-controlled Hip Hop, the poor are targeted by wealthy companies. These companies can afford to have their brand names dropped throughout the hottest artists' albums and throughout the artists' music videos and promotions. This very functional and intentional brand placement stirs up frivolous consumption. It is the association with a known, embraced, and worshipped entertainer, and the visual and audio repetition of the brand that contrives mass consumer interest. An artificial value is assigned to these brands based solely on name recognition and association. And with the assignment of that rigged and inflated value, the poor are willing to pay whatever price to be associated with that brand due to its association with the entertainer. Most times, consumers don't even realize that they love a brand based solely on its being associated with an entertainer they love. The consumer is conned into believing that his/her ravenous consumption is based on his/her individual preference. Either way, the brands win. Through White-owned Black music, White products are sold to drain Black people of their green.

Hop Hop's earlier years were not foreign to the

materialistic. Artist donned name brand track suits, gold chains, and the hottest kicks. The idea was to look as "fly" as possible. Major points were given for originality. Run DMC was among the first to score a lucrative fashion contract. They rocked Adidas, so Adidas saw Run DMC as a portal into the pockets of young Black kids who loved Hip Hop. It worked. Tommy Hilfiger shirts, Troop track suits, Girbaud jeans, and Laura Biagiotti glasses are just a few of the brands that became popular in Hip Hop's earlier years. Some of the brands latched on and made the associations official through contracting the artists. Other brands did not see a need. They sat back and enjoyed the free promotion. Black-owned brands like Dapper Dan and Karl Kani benefitted from Hip Hop exposure as well. The Black brands benefitting from Black kids purveying Black culture is simply family feeding family. Unfortunately, as the commercialization set in, those bonds became fake.

The brand association business in Hip Hop that began organically eventually became a means to mete out the exploitive. The brand placement became more scripted and began to expand beyond clothing. Soon enough, alcohol brands, jewelers, cars, and anything that could be associated with opulence began to litter the Hip Hop landscape. And the names of the brands became more European and way more expensive.

There is a toxic correlation between the advent of "drug dealer rap" and the amounts of expensive European brands flooding rap stanzas. The crack game grew and spread throughout urban areas in the United States in the 1980s and 1990s. Many of the rappers had come up in the drug game and so their bars would be laced with the fancy items they were able to acquire as a direct result of drug profits. Many of the listeners of these rap bars began to see the drug game as a means to cop the expensive items mentioned by their favorite "street reality" rappers. Art imitating life, then life imitating art. Community destruction, family destruction, life destruction, and mass incarceration were the eventual results of the mass promotion of manic materialism without legit means, without legit money. Just another example of the rich preying on the poor. Poor Blacks suffered, aided by well-paid Black pawns from among the poor, while the European owners of Hip Hop and a vast number of European brands got paid. It got to the point where a few rap artists were able to elevate themselves in the rap game, largely based off their willingness to become paid promoters of European brands. Oftentimes, both products and people have price tags. Integrity, principles, and Black pride as hindrances.

A Historical & Sociological Perspective

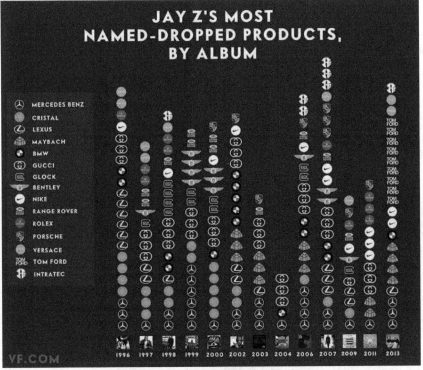

(Vibe.com/Adelle Platon, 2013)

"People get used to anything. The less you think about your oppression, the more your tolerance for it grows. After awhile, people just think oppression is the normal state of things. But to become free, you have to be acutely aware of being a slave."

- Assata Shakur -

We tend not to think of our oppression because we have a myriad of distractions provided by the establishment to keep us occupied, bread and circuses. This is the role of entertainment. Sports, movies, television, social media, and the routines and rituals of our everyday lives keep us more than busy. For too many families and individuals in America and around the world, the struggle of feeding one's self or family is enough to keep the mind occupied. For the employed, by the time we leave a 9 to 5, we have just enough time and energy to small talk with our nuclear families, eat, and prepare for work the next day. Five days on and two days off to enjoy the spoils of wage peonage; leisure time.

Our time is occupied. Most of us don't have time to think about the fact that America is constantly sending young men and women (mostly poor) over to foreign countries to kill and be killed to facilitate the consolidation of the world's resources into fewer hands. Most of us don't have time to think about the fact that in the self-professed "greatest country in the world", millions of children are both homeless and hungry. We don't have time to think about these things, time to care, time to protest, and so these things persist. We don't have time to resist. Very few make time, and so relatively few make it, and many do not, because only a few are meant to. Most of the world's citizens are stuck in impoverished conditions, and the rest are simply provided and satisfied with the distinction of being middle class, which in many cases means a lost job and a couple of missed paychecks away from joining the impoverished global majority.

Economic malaise and resource misallocation are passed on from generation to generation. This world sees monarchs pass huge inheritances, based solely on family blood, down to their entitled children. "Fortunate 500" corporate moguls pass on exploitive corporate plantations down to their silver spoon-tongued young. The employees who toiled and climbed that corporate ladder get to hopefully pass on some property and a little money to their seeds. Many employees manage to ascend that class stratification structure only to see their children must hit reset and start from pocket scratch. That global majority, an unfortunate reality, get to pass on the struggle, the hunger, and the hustle. We are groomed to accept what presents itself a sinister caste system, but "consolation" is, we rarely ever have time to focus attention on it. We rarely are provided the time or the forum to feel the collective pain of the poor, pain buffered by a collective callus; callous. If major media provided us with a clear and unbiased by the wealthy picture of the game and the real players whose wins are predetermined, there would be instant global upheaval, revolutions running amuck. This is why there is the need to funnel and filter the information we receive. Hip Hop used to be a major platform and voice for the voiceless, those with limited choices. The culture's new owners have severely decreased the conversation choices of the artists now under their control. The revolution has been muted.

CHAPTER 12
The Sole Controllers

"Whoever controls the media, the images, controls the culture."

- Allen Ginsberg -

As of 2016, there were six companies that controlled almost all of the media distributed for the entire globe (the number is down to 5 as of 2020). This means that all of the news, music, TV, movies, magazines, and other sorts of media reflect the voices of a small segment of the global population, generally those with the means to facilitate such a consolidation of information. They are National Amusements, Disney, Time-Warner, Comcast, News Corp, and Sony. This list is subject to change at a moment's notice as mergers and consolidations are occurring almost yearly. As of 2012, some combination of these companies has controlled approximately 90% of the world's media distribution. Not only do they get to decide what information we receive, they get to decide how we receive it. In other words, these companies possess the power to dictate perceptions and perspectives through the manipulation of narratives, stories, and images. A handful of companies tell us what to think and how and when to think about it. When our thoughts are being controlled, our actions are as well. Our opinions of people are shaped by these companies. The most dangerous example of this is when these companies use their power to promote polished versions of poisonous politicians to the public. People in America and around the globe generally vote based on how candidates are portrayed via media. Media companies have the power to make or break politicians or anyone for that matter. The media has the power help win an office for a politician and it also has the power to kill an entertainer's career. Media companies get to decide who passes as a hero or is cast a villain. The most mundane of personalities can become an overnight star while a rising star can be toppled in the same amount of time with a few timely, well-placed, choice bits of information. That is a lot of power for six companies to possess, especially in the context of an entire globe.

The biggest priority of those in power across the globe is the maintenance of the status quo. The most effective way to maintain the status quo is through the control of information. The rich control the media. As a result, the rich are portrayed favorably across all mediums to the point where they are embraced, celebrated, and venerated by those who have little and little reason to do so. Those who do not "have" want to become like those who do. Greed is glamorized. Through the same media, the poor and those who do not have quite as much are kept divided, distracted, and focused on everything but the consolidation of the world's wealth by the globe's wealthiest. As capitalism calls for, caste and class systems are neatly maintained by the flow of information. The control of the media is power wielded by the most powerful. The only way to not be subjected to the manipulation and fine-tuning meted out by major media conduits is to lessen consumption of it drastically or simply unplug from it. Most of us are not going to or are unable to totally unplug from these compromised mediums of information. With that, it is probably best that we evolve a thorough understanding of how media works and how it affects us. We all need to become more media literate. Media is a tool and it is also a weapon. We need to be able to discern the difference.

It matters who the chef is. I am quite certain that most of us would hesitate to eat a meal prepared by a chef who had historically proven to be an enemy. The unfortunate reality is that in regard to the media Black people consume, not much of it is actually Black-owned; someone else is preparing our meals. Many times, we're getting another's interpretation of our culture. Many times, we're reading articles or watching television shows and movies that may have been created by Black people, but their perspectives, thoughts, and creativity have been edited or filtered to either water down the messages or to fit certain narratives. This applies to Hip Hop as well. We may get to see our artists and hear their songs, but many times, by the time we get to hear the finished product, it's been augmented to satisfy the agendas and sensibilities of people who don't necessarily have our best interests at heart.

Essence Magazine, a magazine geared toward Black women, was controlled by Time Inc., which owned 49% of the magazine up until 2005. In 2005, Time Inc. bought the remaining 51% of that ownership. Time Inc.'s ownership of Essence magazine lasted until 2018 when it was purchased by a Black-owned company. This means that Essence magazine featured a lot of information edited and infused with a Eurocentric slant. Nothing truly empowering. Ebony, a magazine Africans in America have been leaning on for Black culture for decades, has been owned by JP Morgan Chase. Ironically, Chase bank was involved with the slave trade in America when it was founded and for years afterwards.

"...Citizen's Bank and Canal Bank in Louisiana, both now part of J.P. Morgan, served plantations from the 1830s until the American civil war, which ended in 1865. The banks would take ownership of slaves when the plantation owners defaulted on bank loans. The bank estimated that between 1831 and 1865 the two banks accepted approximately 13,000 slaves as collateral and ended up owning about 1,250 slaves..."

(The Guardian, David Teather, 1/21/2005)

XXL Magazine, a magazine that targets the traditional lovers of Hip Hop, Black youth, is owned by Townsquare Media. Huffington Post: Black Voices is owned by Arianna Huffington. The Root, where many of us garner current events or happenings in the Black community, is owned by Univision. TV One, where we get to watch some of our favorite sitcoms and biographies, is owned by Radio One, which falls under the umbrella of Comcast. BET (Black Entertainment Television) is owned by Viacom which is owned by a Mr. Sumner Redstone. All the aforementioned are White/Jewish-owned entities with their own agendas. We have been forced to subsist from information that does not accurately reflect Black culture, and more often than not, distorts the perceptions of Black people.

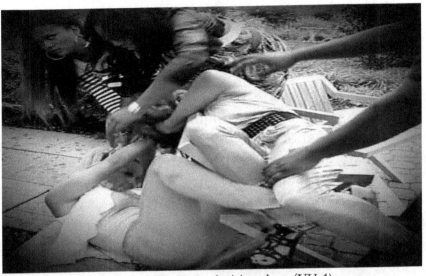

(Love and Hip Hop television show/VH-1)

Context is everything. We are quick to say, "well what's the big deal, so what if we don't own it". Look at it this way. Europeans do not have any media targeting them that is owned and produced by Black people. Why would they? Certain historical, sociological, and economic indiscretions have helped place Europeans in these seats of ownership. We must begin to understand the urgency of our need to change this dynamic. What sensible people would allow others to tell their stories for them? Especially with our stories being repeatedly remixed for distortion and re-definition. Control of our own media needs to be a priority.

We have powerful precedents that serve as beacons for what Black media ownership looks like. Decades after Reconstruction, we were still forced to fend for ourselves and produce everything the Black community needed. Racism and discrimination forced our hands. We could not rely on the altruism of others and so we became autonomous. We thrived. We built homogenous self-contained Black communities all over the United States that featured our own banks, grocery stores, schools, theatres, public transportation, construction, and clothiers. Africans in America had a wealth of talent that we maintained that was brought over to this country from across the Atlantic. We maintained what we had, and mastered other needed skill sets in the years after chattel slavery. Africans had done most of the heavy lifting in building up the South and other parts of the U.S. during slavery. There was no doubt that we possessed the skills and the capacity we needed to build and create for ourselves while adjusting to that cruel institution.

We had our own Black media too. Frederick Douglass established the *North Star* newspaper in 1847 to tackle the issues of slavery abolition. The paper also addressed the emancipation of women and other oppressed groups. He had a circulation of around 4,000 in America, Europe, and the West Indies. Douglas eventually merged his paper with a paper called *The Liberty Party Paper*. It was eventually renamed *Frederick Douglass' Paper*. In 1860, when Douglass discontinued the paper, he published a magazine called the *Douglass' Monthly*. In 1870, he acquired a paper in Washington DC he named *The New National Era* to serve former slaves.

The North Star newspaper (TheWeeklyChallenger.com, 2019)

Pan-Africanist great, Marcus Garvey, understood how necessary it was for us to own our media platforms. In 1918, Marcus Garvey established the *Negro World* newspaper which served as the voice of his United Negro Improvement Association. The paper highlighted issues related to Black nationalism and connected Africans throughout the diaspora. It also gave a voice to Black women with contributions from Garvey's wife, Amy. The *Negro World* was particularly important during the Harlem Renaissance as a platform for Black arts and artists - it provided a forum for Black culture. Garvey's paper had an international distribution of about 500,000 weeklies. Garvey's paper was banned in colonies conquered, occupied, and controlled by Europeans. The last thing they wanted was a population of Africans uplifted and inspired to stand up and fight for their independence. In some instances, The *Negro World* infiltrated these racist barriers when it was smuggled into ports and towns by Black seamen.

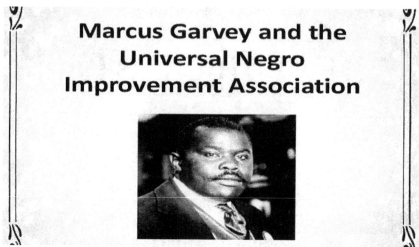

Marcus Garvey and the Universal Negro Improvement Association

(Slideshare.net, 2020)

Conceding the power to define ourselves to others has great potential to negatively impact us psychologically. Imagery is powerful. Unfortunately, this is where we find ourselves today. We see the greatest disparity in Black/White ownership within the realm of media. With respect to the mediums; television, movie, magazines, newspapers, and the internet, Blacks are lagging far behind in terms of being able to define ourselves and being able to tell our own stories. Whites/Jews have the wheel. According to the FCC, Blacks own .6% of television stations. That's a mere 9 or 10 television stations in the entire United States. The watchdog group, Free Press, places the total of Black-owned and operated "full-power" television stations at zero. In 1995, there were 146 radio stations in America owned by Blacks. As of 2015, there were only around 68. Of the 10,000 commercial radio stations in America, less than 1% are Black-owned.

A major reason for the lack of Black representation in radio ownership is Bill Clinton's 1996 Telecommunications Act. Previously, the Federal

Communications Commission (FCC) had policies in place that prevented any single entity from holding more than one broadcast license in the same community. Having a larger more diversified group of owners provided opportunities for more voices to be heard, preferably voices that represented the respective communities. The new law allowed any communications business to compete in any market against one another. Basically, the industry was deregulated allowing single companies to consolidate ownership of multiple media outlets. Wealthy corporations were quick to take advantage of the lack of federal oversight. Black-owned radio stations felt the pain of that consolidation; they were edged out.

Today, we have huge corporate-owned radio stations in every major urban area that targets Black audiences. The overwhelming majority are owned by Europeans/Jews. They feature Black radio personalities, music from Black recording artists, Black community news and updates, and advertisement aimed at Black consumers. All of these stations employ programmers. The radio programmer is the person at the station charged with scheduling the content to be broadcasts from the station. Many of these programmers don't represent the communities they are charged with programming content for. These radio station programmers work for large conglomerates that don't have a vested interest in Black communities and are required to carry out whatever agendas these large wealthy conglomerates may have in play. Most of the music played on these urban stations encourages Black youth to engage in criminal or other self-destructive behaviors. There isn't much, if any, music coming from these stations that encourages, uplifts, or empowers Black youth. Music isn't the only issue, but it's clear that much of what we have the misfortune of seeing and reading daily in the news is a reflection of what our kids listen to. There are plenty of profits to be made from the criminalization of large numbers of Black kids. In America, it always boils down to money. The drive to make major profits is always on the backs of the most vulnerable and powerless segments of the population.

Every second of the day in every urban area that features large populations of Black people, the most vile, toxic, disrespectful, and debasing music is being played by urban radio djs. The "music" is saturated with misogyny, murder, materialism, drug dealing, drug use, and other criminal degenerate behavior. This is the music featured on these stations all day every day. At least 9 times every hour, a young, minimally talented artist is provided a platform to promote the negative "propagandization" of Black people. The devaluation of Black culture on these mediums has been normalized. Not one other ethnic group is "gifted" the opportunity to define themselves as less than via radio. There was never a demand from us to feature music that describes ourselves as "bitches" and "niggas", yet radio executives will tell us that they are just meeting a demand. In actuality, they're just tapping into a supply, artists waiting in line to sign record deals where they get to subjugate their own race even further. The radio executives tell us it's what we like, but in reality, these A&Rs (Artists and Repertoire) and recording executives have been demanding less and less in terms of talent. Hip Hop is being re-defined from the top down, not the other way around. The exact same occurred within other music genres such as Rhythm and Blues and Jazz. The culture is being dumbed down. Any artist can record an album full of barely audible ignorance, and with that bar lowered, many artists now do. More money for the vultures of our culture. We have plenty of genuinely talented artists who don't get airtime on the radio, artists who create music that uplifts, encourages, and empowers, but most urban radio stations won't play them. Why is that? Why are so many of our true artists being censored?

CHAPTER 13
Propaganda

"The mass media serve as a system for communicating messages and
symbols to the general populace. It is their function to amuse, entertain,
and inform, and to inculcate individuals with the values, beliefs, and codes
of behavior that will integrate them into the institutional structures of the
larger society. In a world of concentrated wealth and major conflicts of
class interest, to fulfill this role requires systematic propaganda."

- Noam Chomsky -

Propaganda is psychological conditioning. When we tune
in to the nightly news with regularity and view the
gratuitous images of Blacks being mistreated, beaten, and
killed, we tend to become desensitized to the plight of the
Black collective who are the subjects of a disproportionate
amount of abuse from America's state-sanctioned
authority. After awhile the "shock value" diminishes and
we come to view these occurrences as just the way things
are. The nonsensical is normalized. Once we are
completely desensitized to these events, we are less likely
to mount a meaningful or effective response to curb them.
Our collective inaction is unnatural, but we are primed to
accept certain unfortunate realities. With the advent of
cell phone videos, Black death has become akin to
American porn, something to watch for a quick hit of
delight. The thrill of the kill.

Propaganda is subconscious programming. The
subconscious mind has more control over our conscious
actions than the conscious mind. It is the subconscious
mind that processes what we take in as stimulus every
moment we're awake. It's what we've processed via our

five senses. The subconscious also processes the messages we take in subliminally and oftentimes, these are the most potent. Product advertisers spend millions of dollars infusing their commercials and advertisements with hidden messages, messages only hidden from our eyes. The finished products of our subconscious mind's consumption are our guiding thoughts. Our actions and behaviors are dictated by the thoughts manifested from our subconscious. We can think of the subconscious mind as the operating system of a computer. It is how we're hardwired. Within our subconscious mind are housed our personalities, behaviors, and habits, the things that drive us. Many of the things we do involuntarily or without realizing we're doing them are the manifestations of our subconscious programming. Often, we perceive these actions as conscious choices, not understanding the work that our subconscious programming played in our preferences.

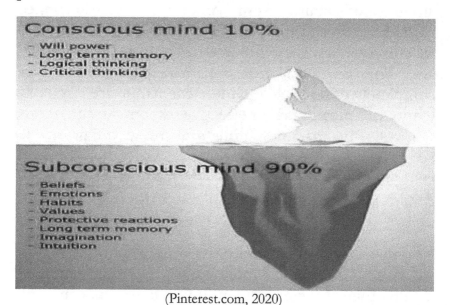

(Pinterest.com, 2020)

The subconscious can be programmed for positive behavior such as the consumption of media that encourages healthy eating. Alternatively, the subconscious can be rendered toxic. For example, young people consume gratuitous amounts of negative propaganda, veiled as music, which suggests to them that all peer conflict is to be settled with some sort of violent or deadly reaction. The following excerpt is from a song entitled *Life is Good.*

". .I put you face on the news,

I put the p*ssy on the shirt.

After I murk,

Then make 'em go shoot up the hearse.

Cost me a quarter-bird,

N*gga it's worth it.

Then you a maniac. ."

- Future (featuring Drake) –

Translated, the lyrics refer to the act of murdering someone so their face can be viewed on the news. The lyrics suggest that the murder victim's face will then adorn the ubiquitous, spray-painted t-shirts that get made, featuring the victim's cartooned face along with the abbreviation, R.I.P. The rapped bars continue with a reference to shooting up the murder victim's funeral after paying someone ¼ of a kilogram of cocaine for their sinister service. This sort of sonic toxicity is now the rule all over urban radio, available and accessible to anyone with a radio 24/7. When the mass consumption of negative propaganda is partnered with environmental depravity, depression, and disenfranchisement, often the results contribute to criminality which feeds the criminal justice system and helps cement the status quo. The obvious correlation is deafening but the cries to stop the targeting of youth, specifically Black youth, with destructive media continue to go unheeded.

From birth, we all have a subconscious that has been inputted with great amounts of what would be considered behavior modification. Our behaviors and habits are largely dictated by what we see and hear from family, peers, schools, and the media. America has a set of desired behaviors it seeks from the American populace. America prefers its citizens blindly patriotic, entertainment-addicted, materialistic, and somewhat dimwitted. It does not serve America's ruling elite to have a population rife with critical thinking human beings. Critical thinkers ask insightful questions armed with information they'd sought out themselves, versus allowing themselves to be spoon-fed information from mainstream sources. A population of informed people would demand answers to the questions they pose. They would dig for the truth and assert that truth about their individual and collective rights and right to liberty. They would be a lot harder to program and manage. It would be exponentially harder to continue to exploit and steal from a population of analytical thinkers who question and research all information with due discernment. Revolutions occur when information received by the oppressed awakens them to the realities of their oppression. These collective revolts serve the purpose of toppling the system that has deceived and exploited them. From the dust, they rebuild and create a system that is more just. As it stands today, we are programmed to accept capitalism, imperialism, militarism, and racism. African people are programmed for self-loathing and self-hatred. African youth, in many regards, are programmed to self-destruct. African subjugation serves the status quo construct.

Propaganda is what renders our entertainment a weapon of sorts. We generally view entertainment as something to be enjoyed in our leisure time. While being entertained, we tend to relax and surrender our minds. Entertainment is among the ways we escape from our often-mundane realities. We generally don't feel the compulsion to analyze what we're being entertained by. Again, the focus is on escape and enjoyment. It is amidst these mental retreats that our minds are the most vulnerable. This is when the weaponized nature of propaganda is most effective.

On the battlefield that is psychological warfare, propaganda is the most potent weapon employed by those in power. Prolonged wars often feature multiple battles with different phases and types of engagement. Africans in America and across the globe have been the targets of war for centuries. From the time the Portuguese first touched down in West Africa as veiled antagonists up through today, Europeans have been subjecting African people to a hell-infused reality. Our focus is mostly concerned with survival.

Europeans invaded the African continent and eventually contrived economic cause to capture African people for the purpose of shipping us across the Atlantic Ocean to work as human property on plantations throughout the Americas, the West Indies, and Europe. The nature of the war against Black people has morphed since that time from forced labor on plantations into forced labor in prisons per mass incarceration politics and policies. The methods and tactics have changed, but the oppression, subjugation, and exploitation persist. Those in power have applied fresh coats of paint to our continued exploitation to render it more palatable. Many of us have even found comfort within its constraints.

The best way to continue to wage a genocidal campaign against a group of people with minimal pushback is to do so without most of that group realizing war is occurring. Propaganda is the biggest cannon in that effort. The war against us never ceased, we have just been socialized to find a comfortable seat within it.

America's war is not just against African people who continue to find themselves in last place in every measurable category of growth, it is also being waged against the nation's poor. We find ourselves confused and continually voting for leaders who do nothing but perpetuate our pain. That propaganda arm is strong. Only a weapon as strong as America's information apparatus could get people to continuously vote and act against their own interests for decades. We continuously find ourselves complicit in the maintenance of the status quo. The rich stay rich while the poor blindly support systems, institutions, and policies that keep them poor. The way it's set up though, African people in America, as a collective, have constantly found themselves languishing in last in that bottom caste. That boot on our backs keeping us pinned to the bottom isn't as easily identifiable as the leg and foot powering that boot. It's clear who our oppressors are but we need to become worlds more adept at identifying their methods and machinery.

Conspiracy - a secret plan by a group to do something unlawful or harmful.

We live in a society that is quick to dismiss those who formulate theories that paint pictures of the invisible hands and strings conducting our everyday lives. We want to believe what we're told by major media sources because it removes the onus from us of having to qualify the information for ourselves. As a society, we are being taught that if one doesn't succeed, or even an entire group of people aren't succeeding, it's the fault of that individual or group. We're great at absolving those who actually conspire for the sake of consolidating the wealth of the nation and world. Conscientiously proposed conspiracies require unquestionable proof while the nightly news is subject to immediate approval from us. We tend not to accept the existence of conspiracies until the often-deadly desired results have already been achieved.

One need not be a conspiracy theorist to draw the conclusion that there are apparatuses in place to prevent the collective ascendancy of African people in America. Any denial of conspiracies in this vein reinforce the belief that African people are innately or inherently failures who relish the opportunities disenfranchisement avails to us. This is the mindset of both the racist and the African who has been rendered anti-African by racist propaganda.

Conspiracies aside, we need to understand that war isn't always abject, unadulterated violence. The less sophisticated attacks against us saw us lynched, beheaded, burned, raped, whipped, beaten, and shot. Today's efforts are far more tactical and strategic. War is carried out through systems and mechanisms of control. This sort of warfare is worlds easier because it solicits and garners the acceptance of those the war is being waged against.

We see ourselves as winning as we embrace and indulge the weaponry we are targeted with. We're fed, clothed, educated, medicated, and entertained by the instruments of Black genocide. We've embraced consumerism and materialism. We spend as we've been socialized to, in a manner that enriches others exponentially more than we contribute to our own economic growth. We've had a history of not having which dictates to us that we wear our status as a reflection of the progress we believe has been made. Individualism and individual achievements have taken precedent over the success of the community. "Look at me" is our mantra.

Food is survival. We're targeted with foods that put significant dents in our lifelines. We have inherited a gamut of debilitating and deadly diseases as a direct result of the foods we were forced to eat on plantations that have somehow matriculated into our contemporary eating habits. Black people are disproportionally more predisposed to strokes and heart disease than Whites. Black men have higher rates of prostate cancer than White men. That genetic predisposition to these diseases is directly attributed to the foods we eat and pass down generationally, often as tradition. America's capitalist-controlled FDA (Food and Drug Administration) cares little for American people to begin with. This especially applies for those people who weren't intended to be recognized as full citizens to begin with.

Our integration into America's schools is seeing us integrated and assimilated as our sense of self-respect, our autonomy, and our culture is being evaporated. Martin Luther King intimated towards the end of his life that he may have been "integrating us into a burning house". We've been aflame and affixed to the idea of inclusion and acceptance ever since. We surrendered our autonomy and settled for affirmative action. Those who don't eventually disengage from the education process here find themselves saturated with the Eurocentric, but very little if any Afro-centric. School serves the purpose of making full-fledged Americans out of us at the expense of our true selves. We rarely return to that. We attend schools and achieve varying degrees of accomplishment that reflect our specified levels of certification and training, very little education.

The education a people receive is supposed to empower them. At present, we have very little power. The African enrolled in America's schools accepts degrees in lieu of that self-sustaining power. Our employment numbers have always been low in comparison to other groups due to discrimination and other societal factors, but a good number of us have had access to good-paying jobs. However, having a job doesn't necessarily equip one with the mindset or the means to trickle down anything of tangible value to those we often fashion ourselves leaving behind. There are plenty of us employed in various capacities and fields, yet our communities are subject to being white-washed and gentrified in every urban area across the United States today. Again, America's schools do not empower African people.

I'm not among the voices telling African children not to go

to college. I am, however, among the folks who realize that one can attain any number of degrees and letters behind a name and not possess a very necessary knowledge of him or herself. That lack of knowledge leaves one susceptible to becoming just another status quo tool, an educated fool.

We played a major part in the establishment of America's medical industry. We were the guinea pigs and lab rats used in sadistic experiments.

"..Marion Sims, a White man, is considered to be the father of gynecology. In the 19th century, he performed surgical experiments on enslaved Black women without anesthesia.."

(The Washington Post, DeNeen L. Brown, 8/29/2017).

It is ironic that we were not viewed or treated as human beings but were the subjects of these experiments due to our striking resemblance to the humanity they stole from us. Without any sort of anesthesia, Black women's private parts were cut and carved on by wicked doctors who saw them as far less than human. African people were sold to different Whites for the expressed purpose of medical experimentation. Throughout the years, Black people have been purposely infected with various diseases just to plot the courses of these diseases. The infections of loved ones and multiple deaths were the expected and accepted results. Despite this history of well-documented savagery, we continue to place full faith in America's medical professionals, medicines, and facilities. We willfully allow doctors to inject us with all sorts of "FDA-approved for large-scale experiments on human beings" vaccines. Our dependence on America's hospitals is largely due to the same 60's integration bills that see us struggling in de facto segregated schools. Blacks in America are governed by a different set of unfair rules.

Lastly, too many of us don't understand the use and purpose of propaganda, mostly because its cleverly disguised as entertainment. Many of us ignore the existence of it. If I'm your historical enemy and I want to poison you, I'm not going to hand you a bottle with skull and crossbones on it and ask you to drink the bottle's contents. If I find out you love chocolate donuts, I'm going to cook that poison into the best chocolate donut ever. More than likely, to avoid any chance of you refusing to eat it, I'm going to have it gifted to you by someone you trust. Major studios and media distributors like Disney, Sony, and Fox do this quite often with their employment of Black directors, producers, and writers. We trust the cooks, but we don't know the chefs or anyone else in that food distribution chain. We've eaten box after box of those chocolate donuts over the years and many of us are beginning to recognize and realize the manifestations of the covertly concealed poison we've enjoyed consuming. Like many debilitating diseases, self-hatred sets in gradually over time. Much of the media we consume as entertainment is infused with copious amounts of self-loathing to infect the viewer and the listener. Poverty is a major predictor of crime, but so is mental illness. Black children have to be programmed to disregard, dismiss, devalue, and kill one another. That programming is pushed daily through the earbuds parents often find difficulty separating their children from. It's happening through what's presented to our youth as entertainment. It's happening through TV and the movies. It's happening through the music.

"We're the only people on the entire planet who have been taught to sing and praise our demeaning. 'I'm a bitch, I'm a hoe, I'm a gangster, I'm a thug, I'm a dog.' If you can train people to demean and degrade themselves, you can oppress them forever. You can even program them to kill themselves and they won't even understand what happened."

- Dr. Frances Cress Welsing -

We all want to be entertained. The regimented nature of our lives in this capitalist society demands that we have some mechanism that removes our minds from an often rigid, unrelenting reality. For many, that reality is that we're merely surviving, rarely actually living. Entertainment functions as a means to distract us from the monotony of our lives. We often use entertainment as a means to connect with our imaginations. We escape in fairy tales of romance, science fiction, action adventures, cerebral thrillers, and horror movies. Entertainment for many serves as a sedative that helps maintain sanity in a profoundly insane world.

Another benefit of entertainment is that it puts people to work. All communities host a great number of artistically inclined individuals who make a living from some aspect of the entertainment industry. For many it's a hobby, for some it's a job.

Mediums such as television and movies also serve as a reflection of the societies that produce them. They showcase the good and the evil that exist in any society. People relate to the situations and scenarios they view in sitcoms. A lot of what's provided is meant to engage our emotions. It's meant to make us laugh which is among the biggest relievers of stress. We gravitate to programs we can relate to. We see ourselves in our favorite actors and actresses and often enough, mimic them. We're even saddened when certain TV or movie series come to an end. Entertainment is very necessary.

Entertainment influences people's opinions and preferences. This is the propaganda component. Much of what we think is borne of media we've consumed. Our choices in fashion, foods, and what we do for fun are often a function of what our minds are fed from media mediums. TV stations receive the bulk of their funding from advertisers so therefore the TV programs are secondary to the ads featured. The focus of TV stations is to make certain their advertising is tactfully targeted towards certain groups of consumers. They expect specific demographics to be watching based on the programming offered. Women are told what to buy during romantic comedies. Men are told what they should spend their money on during televised football games. During these sporting events, both men and women are inputted with American patriotism and pageantry. The American flag and anthem are featured at the beginning of every sporting event. Soldiers are seated strategically in arenas. Commercials are purposely placed at game time-outs and other breaks in action. Marketing is a multi-billion-dollar industry. Every commercial and every message, subliminal or obtuse, is positioned with a purpose. Our thoughts and, as a corollary, our behaviors, are shaped by these well-placed media components.

Black people in America have been the victims of decades of these well-placed components. How we view ourselves, each other, and how the world views us is largely the result of mass media. Stigmatizing imagery and narratives have gradually taken their psychological toll on us. Through American mass media, we started as the savages, subservient beasts, and morons depicted by White face-painters on the big screen at the turn of the 20th century. From there, we continued as Black actors who were only cast as savages, subservient beasts, and morons. We also got to be cast in cartoons where we were animated savages, subservient beasts, and morons. We are now amidst several eras of television and movies where we have willfully embraced roles in Hollywood as savages, subservient beasts, and morons. Spinning our wheels.

Our emergence in entertainment has seen us create, produce, direct, and act in historically decrepit roles that depict us as only a fraction of our total humanity. The reality is that for many Black artists to be employed in the entertainment industry, we have to accept roles that promote images, narratives, and stories that project a very narrow version of the Black experience. Gang member roles are disproportionately filled by Black actors. Zachary Crockett of Vox Magazine observed 160,000 acting credits from 26,000 films and found that the "thug" roles were filled by Black men 66% of the time. This was in 2016. Not much has changed in the last four years. Black artists are often forced to belittle themselves and their people for the sake of being employed entertainers. This reflects the fact that Black people do not own major production studios or any of the major distribution needed to get one's work seen by large numbers of people. We have to pander to poisonous propaganda agendas in order to see a profit. The fact that only a debased version of the African experience is welcome on major media platforms is evidence of the fact that there is an agenda to maintain America's caste system as it historically and currently exists, with Blacks on the bottom. In any given summer, you will find White actors and actresses cast as all sorts of heroes, heroines, and whole people. During these same summers, you'll likely find Blacks cast in very typical roles; savages, subservient beasts, and morons. The function of entertainment is to make us feel good, but it also serves the purpose of maintaining societal stratifications. It's important we begin to understand how entertainment serves as propaganda, so we're not continuously exploited by it. Entertainment is to be enjoyed, but we should never surrender our minds to it for the sake of that enjoyment. We should be clear on its function. That function is control.

Left: World War I propaganda poster, 1918. Right: Vogue magazine cover featuring Lebron James and Gisele Bundchen.

"If you can control a man's thinking you do not have to worry about his action. When you determine what a man shall think, you do not have to concern yourself about what he will do. If you make a man feel that he is inferior, you do not have to compel him to accept an inferior status, for he will seek it himself. If you make a man think that he is justly an outcast, you do not have to order him to the back door. He will go without being told; and if there is no back door, his very nature will demand one."

- Carter G. Woodson -

CHAPTER 14
Clandestine Acts

Is there a secretive, secluded group of wealthy Whites or Jews who expend energy and effort towards the extermination of Black people? Are there systems and policies in play for the sole purpose of Black genocide? The proof is in the precedents. When we hear the word holocaust, we immediately associate it with the historical accounts of Jews being exterminated in Nazi Germany during World War II. Rarely does the word holocaust initiate thoughts of the less talked about but well-documented accounts of King Leopold's and Cecil Rhode's mass exterminations of millions of Africans in the Congo and Zimbabwe. These were major holocausts that, attrition wise, far exceeded that of the Jewish holocaust. Both saw the tragic, unfortunate, and unnecessary loss of human lives.

There's a difference though between these two genocidal campaigns in regard to their respective residual effects. The Jewish community has more than recovered, while Africans are still reeling from the longstanding effects of continued oppression, occupation, and neo-colonization. We rarely hear the word genocide being applied to the African captives living in America. Africans were transported to this country from West African shores to the Americas as property to be bought and sold. The life of an African slave held value that was solely attached to his/her value to the institution of chattel slavery, never value attached to his/her humanity. Not much has changed. An African in this country can still be murdered by "slave-catchers" who often escape prosecution in the media and the courts. These individuals seem to possess tort immunity. The scale is still unbalanced.

When slavery ended in 1865, it didn't. The enslavement of African people after the 13th amendment continued unabated. It has undergone several phases, each rendering it a bit prettier, more polished, but just as productive and profitable. Sharecropping, Black Codes, chain gangs, Jim Crow laws, and mass incarceration have all had the exact same crippling effect on Black people in America. They all looked eerily the same; policies that railroad Black people into jail to be exploited for cheap labor, leaving families and communities broken by the hemorrhaging of its Black men and women from those communities.

(Chain Gang, Robert E. Ireland, 2006)

The Black holocaust is still happening, however its worlds more subtle, it's systemic. Genocide is built into just about every major policy or institution affecting Black people. It's in the food, it's in the healthcare and medicines we're prescribed, it's in the schools, and it's in the predatory financial institutions. It's in neighborhood residency reallocations and restrictions that find us hoarded into high concentration areas of concentrated poverty where government officials concentrate on incarcerating us. The media we embrace as entertainment is saturated with Black genocide. That last piece is the least acknowledged, but probably the most formidable. You don't have to worry about a man's actions when you control his mind. We consume massive amounts of media distributed by people who don't look like us, who hate us, and who have had a lengthy record of exploiting us.

Right up there with media, the history of Black genocide through medicines is well-documented. From 1932 to 1972, Black men were unknowingly experimented on by the United States department of Public Health in concert with Tuskegee University, a historically Black college in Alabama. The researchers recruited Black men who were diagnosed with syphilis and then, unknown to the test subjects, administered placebos to counter their diagnoses. The U.S. government used Black men as lab rats to map the deadly progression of the disease through their bodies. Countless STD-stricken Black men suffered and died, and an untold number went on to infect their wives or sex partners, spreading the disease exponentially through families and communities. There is no telling how many additional people died as an indirect result of those men being allowed to unknowingly spread the deadly disease to others.

From 1945 to 1956, the American government, in concert with The Rockefeller Foundation and John Hopkins University, purposely infected hundreds of Guatemalans with STDs such as syphilis and gonorrhea to determine the effects of various drugs on the diseases. The U.S. government was willing to risk the health and the lives of Guatemalans to determine if penicillin could prevent the diseases from occurring. Much like the Tuskegee Experiment, not only the immediate test subjects were victimized, but their families and communities suffered greatly as well. In 2015, over 800 plaintiffs filed a class-action suit against John Hopkins University for the horrendous damage inflicted upon them.

In 1971, a group of activists broke into one of the FBI's Pennsylvania offices. The group stole more than 1,000 FBI documents that exposed years of the U.S. government's efforts, through the Federal Bureau of Investigation, to derail any groups considered legitimate threats to America's status quo. The stolen papers revealed that the United States covertly housed an agenda that featured the dissolution of any groups challenging America's debilitating and oppressive domestic and foreign policies. The FBI's COINTELPRO (Counterintelligence Program) specialized in wiretappings, organization infiltrations, and media manipulation. Most of the COINTELPRO objectives focused on progressive Black organizations such as the S.N.C.C, (Student Non-Violent Coordinating Committee) the S.C.L.C. (Southern Christian Leadership Conference), the C.O.R.E. (Congress of Racial Equality), and the Black Panthers. COINTELPRO also sought to undermine individuals such as Medgar Evers, Malcolm X, and Martin

Luther King. Many of the members of progressive Black organizations, like the the aforementioned, were set up or assassinated by the U.S. government or U.S. agents. The murders of Black Panther Party members Fred Hampton and Mark Clark were orchestrated by the U.S. as part of the FBI's COINTELPRO. There is a book, "The COINTELPRO Papers' by Ward Churchill and Jim Vander Wall that details many of the U.S. COINTELPRO efforts to disrupt dissent.

(The COINTELPRO Papers (front cover), Churchill and Wall, South End Press, 1990)

Many Black communities in the U.S. are plagued with poverty, on purpose. A lot of our communities are saturated with drugs, guns, dysfunction, and crime. The extent of the existence of these unfortunate elements in Black communities is rooted in government efforts to disrupt and destabilize them. The U.S. government, as a component of what came to be known as the Iran-Contra Affair, delivered tons of cocaine into depressed and depraved communities of Black people to be converted into crack which has continued to ravage Black communities throughout America to this day.

The Iran-Contra Affair took place in the 1980s during Ronald Reagan's tenure as the President of the United States. In short, it involved secret and illegal weapons transactions and other covert activities that involved the exchanges of weapons, money, and drugs. The United States, Israel, Iran, and Nicaragua were the main countries involved. Although a number of U.S. government organizations and officials were implicated, Ronald Reagan never admitted to any involvement. Gary Webb was the journalist who provided the bulk of incriminating evidence and indictments with information provided by individuals directly involved. He was later found dead of a gunshot wound, no motives, no suspects.

The crack cocaine epidemic that the Iran-Contra Affair launched saw many Black men hoisted off to prison. It saw many fall prey to addiction and death, and it proved to be the most destabilizing factor in Black communities the last 2 or 3 decades. The 80's and the 90's also saw the production of music which promoted the enterprise of crack dealing, actually glamorizing it. Many young Black males came to see dealing crack as a means of rising above poverty, most persuaded by both their conditions and artists who used their platforms to purvey that message.

The World Knows

In 1951, a group known as the Civil Rights Congress appealed to the United Nations to charge the United States government with genocide against Black people in America. The petition cited the numerous slayings of Blacks by Whites and White police officers, lives deliberately hampered and hindered through the cultivation of conditions that promoted premature death, poverty, and disease. The group referenced the United Nations Convention on the Prevention and Punishment of the Crime of Genocide. As previously mentioned, we often see genocide as the complete extermination of a group of people but the meaning as defined by the United Nations is a bit broader. In 1948, the United Nations defined genocide as any killings on the basis of race, but also, "causing serious bodily or mental harm to members of the group". The definition also incorporates "consistent, conscious, unified policies of every branch of government." America qualifies.

In 2011, another group under the name, We Charge Genocide, appealed to the United Nations on behalf of Black people in the United States, again citing America's systemic oppression and inequality. Genocide is "the deliberate killing of a large group of people, especially those of a particular ethnic group" (Oxford Dictionary). The group made mention of the continuing pattern of violence and the murders of Blacks and Latinos by Chicago police officers. The U.N. condemned these race-based acts of violence and demanded accountability from the agencies responsible. At the U.N., it was determined that genocide is not just limited to killings. Genocide also applies to the mass incarcerating of Black men. Black men are incarcerated at a rate exponentially that of White men. According to the U.S. Bureau of Justice, in 2018, Black men accounted for 34% of the total male prison population. White men accounted for 29% of the prison population. According to the same data, Black people are only about 13% of the total population. Less than half of that 13% is Black men. White males are between 30% and 35% of the total U.S. population. These numbers are absurd.

The "school-to-prison pipeline" is mentioned in that United Nations report. It details how Black student incidents of misbehavior are criminalized far more often than that of our White counterparts. This criminalization and stigmatization, in addition to other precipitating factors, often places students on paths out of school and into the criminal justice system. The same way propaganda primed Jews for extermination by the Nazis, Black people are prepared for prison through criminalization. Just listen to any urban radio station targeting Black audiences and take a gander at what passes as music; listen to the messages.

CHAPTER 15
The New Blackface

Bert Williams was a Bahamian-American and one of the first Blacks to land a role in an American motion picture. Pictured wearing blackface in 1921.
(Longreads.com, 2018)

Many of us venture into restaurants and fast food establishments and consume food without a second thought about who prepares the food. We eat and we trust that the foods we eat will not leave us ill (or deceased). We trust our local municipalities to adequately inspect restaurants to ensure that they are up to code. By the same notion, we consume media from various mediums throughout the day without a second thought as to who delivers it to us. We're addicted. We consume it for the salt and the sugar, the tasty processed and artificial flavors, the inorganic, the entertainment "value". We don't lend a second thought to ingredients like agendas or well-placed propaganda. We're rarely in tune with the often-subtle imagery or narratives being purveyed. If it tastes good or makes us feel good, we eat it up. We have devolved a palate for self-destructive fare.

Portrait of a Paradigm Shift

"As far as the content that we are dealing with in the music today, that came about, in my opinion, as a way of redirecting or putting leads on the people's impulse to pursue revolution. They put leads in the form of gangster rap, pimpism, and hustlin' culture on the people's impulse for revolution to direct them into a self-destructive mindset and that's where we are at right now. We are in that self-destructive mindset that the people went into based on leads that were put on that original impulse and desire to seek revolution. And it was planned. It was definitely planned. I was there when the transition was coming forth. The Poor Righteous Teachers were signed to Profile Records and Profile Records had a couple of conscious groups and then they had Run D.M.C. and so on and so forth. But in the era of gangster rap, we saw DJ Quik come in, we saw N 2 Deep come in, we saw Smooth Da Hustler come in at Profile Records, we saw these things happening right before our eyes. We saw the marketing dollars being redirected from the positive or socially conscious groups to the gangster rapper. We saw these things happening. One thing that the 10% know is that whatever a person thinks, that will become their reality. Whatever a person thinks and believes to be true, that will become their surroundings. And the 10% knew that Hip-Hop was very, very powerful in that era. We had youth braiding their hair up, wearing Afros, putting on their medallions. We were just seeking knowledge in all forms everywhere. And they saw this and they knew that they had to stop this. So Counter Intelligence Programs (COINTELPRO) came into effect and we got what we got and we have what we have today. That pretty much is the process in what happened in Hip-Hop. We have to understand today. You know a lot of people like to say that the artist is responsible, the artist shouldn't say this. I am not taking blame off of individuals that contribute to the self-destructive content in their music. But it is almost like blaming Jezebel for being born poor, but beautiful. It is almost like that (beauty) is the only thing she has to reach out and get the necessities that she needs. You know, the bare necessities. So she is using what she got to get what she wants pretty much. And that is the science with poor people. Poor people can be controlled by the rich. There is a scripture in Proverbs that says, "It is the rich that cause the poor to sin". Because the rich can make a poor man do anything for the bare necessities. And that is what the youth are. The youth are poor, living in poverty and want of all things. And when you are in such a condition it is easy for you to be led in the wrong direction. When poor youth thought that they could rhyme positive socially and politically conscious lyrics and get record deals and sell records like Public Enemy, like KRS-One, like Poor Righteous Teachers, like X-Clan, they were doing it. The large majority of rappers were writing in a conscious format. Yet when they saw the shift, the youth made the shift also. Because they felt, "oh I can't get paid no more doing that, so I have to do this." It is just like how at one point in my neighborhood, everybody was selling marijuana, everybody was selling weed. Everybody. When crack came in 1982 and 1983 to my neighborhood, and they saw that crack was making more money, and there were more crack smokers than weed smokers. Weed wasn't making enough money and they started selling crack. That's what the poor kids do. They are going to do those things that they feel will get them what they desire."

- Wise Intelligent - Poor Righteous Teachers -

Wise Intelligent reinforces what various rap artists over the years have articulated. The industry is now controlled by record companies and record company executives who no do not value Hip Hop culture. Hip Hop empowered an entire generation of Black youth to seek the truth about themselves, the world, and their place within this world. It was cool to be a smart kid. It was cool to read books. It was cool to embrace Africa and the cultural and material vestiges of one's own roots. There have been artists besides Wise Intelligent who have elaborated on their attempts to do conscious records only to have them dismissed by record executives who demand that they only continue to promote and glorify ignorance. Scarface is among a handful of rappers who acknowledged that the paradigm in rap was shifting and that it was not necessarily a shift being cued by those of the culture.

There was never a demand for the glorification of abject negativity in Hip Hop. We didn't ask for what is being supplied to us. Basic economics dictates that it is demand that determines supply, but the situation in Hip Hop is a bit more complicated. There was never a time in Hip Hop history that Black youth, as a collective, screamed out, "we want more ignorance, misogyny, and murder in rap music!" That never happened. When we were being fed Public Enemy, Poor Righteous Teachers, KRS-1, and Brand Nubian, we ate; we cleaned our plates. The thing is, choices, or demands, are determined by the music industry, an industry that sees industry employees paying radio programmers to get records played. The record industry and the radio are essentially controlled by the same people, more on that later. When the radio consumer is provided with a succinct list of 10 songs to listen to every hour of the day, those choices are whittled down substantially from what actually exists in regard to available music. We are presented with illusory options from which to demand. Had radio continued to play more quality conscious music as part of its daily format, consumers would only have the option of choosing or demanding from among those songs. Today, consumers only have choices from among a slew of negative, self-destructive offerings; the ultimate rigged elections. Demand is contrived in this case. The deal is sweetened with danceable catchy beats and choruses. If the same catchy beats and choruses are applied to conscious rap music, its young listeners extract the exact same enjoyment, as previous generations of Hip Hop heads once did. Those who co-opted Hip Hop, choked the supply, providing us with what they desire us to have access to. Today, in order to listen to conscious rap, in most cases, you have to seek it out. What used to be rap's gritty underground is now rap's conscious community, buried under a fake, fragile foundation that promotes Hip Hop as a weapon to debase Black people. We didn't flip the script; it was flipped on us. We never demanded what exist as Hip Hop today, many of us simply settled for what was being supplied.

Those who defined the new demand for us now own Hip Hop at every level. That ownership enables them to decide what the supply of Hip Hop and the demand for it look like.

Vertical integration in economics is when "a company owns different businesses in the same chain of production and distribution. When a company expands its business into areas that are at different points on the same production path, such as when a manufacturer owns its supplier and distributor." (Investopedia, 6/14/2020) Demand can be both contrived and manipulated in a business utilizing the vertical integration model. The music industry employs this model. Radio djs play music as prompted by radio programmers. Radio programmers are provided with formats and playlists from radio executives who are paid by recording industry executives to make sure certain artists get played continuously. Recording companies are owned by large corporations that also own movie, television, and magazine mediums. They use these mediums to promote their artists. Our demand for music presents itself as whittled down choices from what's offered via a pay-to-play dynamic most of us are unaware of. Once the demand for an abbreviated array of music is established, so is the definition of what qualifies as quality music. Black youth did not decide that lyricism was no longer important in Hip Hop, record executives did. If the standard of what qualifies as Hip Hop is diluted and watered down, the culture is gradually looked upon as one that possesses no viability beyond profitability. It's no longer a credible culture, it's just a fleeting commodity. Anyone can do it and it can be easily replaced. *Voila!*

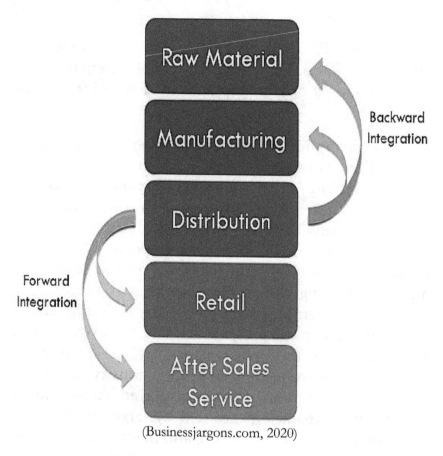

(Businessjargons.com, 2020)

"If Hip Hop has the ability to corrupt young minds, it also has the ability to uplift them"

- KRS-1 -

CHAPTER 16
Conditioning

"You can't listen to all that language and filth without it affecting you"

- C. Delores Tucker -

There is absolutely no way a Black person can consume years, months, weeks, or days worth of negative media portraying and promoting Black men and women as immoral, ignorant, savage, vulgar, and barbaric and not in some way internalize these images. The person who believes this is possible does not totally grasp how propaganda and subliminal messaging works. While we're conscious we don't realize the impact of the gratuitous consumption of toxic messages. We are not supposed to, but the subconscious absorbs these images and narratives like a sponge. Eventually, the behavior desired by the purveyors of the messages are manifested.

Most of the propaganda we ingest is cleverly cloaked as entertainment. I call it the propaganda "trojan horse". On the outside, it's a gift to be embraced, but in reality, its waged war in disguise. First, attack how Blacks view themselves and one another. Secondly, dehumanize and demonize Blacks in the eyes of others. These attacks devalue Black people and render them deserving of whatever strife they are targeted with. The only people actively combating Black genocide are Black people. Relatively few of us understand the need to do so. The army defending the minds of Black youth from these sonic attacks is a small one.

In 2020, a lot of us in America and around the globe proudly refer to ourselves and one another as "niggas". This is the most potent and obvious example of psychological conditioning. For context, consider what would happen if White children or White adult audiences were provided with ample amounts of music, movies, and television programming where they got to hear Whites refer to other Whites as "honkeys' or "crackers", 24 hours a day, 7 days a week. After some time, there's no doubt we'd hear those words tossed between White people in public spaces at an alarming clip. Unfortunately, this situation has only held true for Black people.

Not only have we come to identify ourselves as niggas, or the hyper-masculine, "real niggas", but Black men have grown extremely comfortable referring to Black women as "bitches", cued by European-owned Black entertainment. Black female artists have "empowered" Black women to refer to themselves as bitches, bad and bossy. The Black community has become one saturated with self-professed niggas and bitches. How'd we go from being subjugated, debased, and disrespected by the most detestable word in the English language to embracing it and wearing it as a badge of honor? How did so many sisters go from slapping the taste out of a brother's mouth for directing the word "bitch" at her to proudly placing it on t-shirts and owning it? "If you can make a man think that he is justly an outcast, you do not have to order him to go to the back door. . .he will go without being told; and if there is no back door, his very nature will demand one." Through systemic *miseducation,* we've been well-tooled to build our own back doors. At this juncture, far too many of us are mistaking the back door for a front entrance.

Frequently, I hear the cliché employed, "speak it into existence!" This is an acknowledgement of the power words possess. Words possess tremendous power, especially those we use to define ourselves. We'd have to be completely naive to believe that the television, movie and recording industries aren't aware of this fact.

"Words cannot change reality, but they can change how people perceive reality. Words create filters through which people view the world around them. A single word can make the difference between liking a person and disliking that person."

- Jack Schafer Ph.D. -

Imagine a situation where you are about to be introduced to a person by a friend and the friend refers to the person you are about to meet as being an untrustworthy gossiper. You may not know a single thing about this person you are about to meet, but rest assured, the seed of distrust has already been planted. Despite how genuine and nice this person may be, he or she would have to do a yeoman's job initial introduction and character-wise to erase that forewarning. You will forever be careful with what you mention or do around this person. All it took was the words "untrustworthy gossiper" as applied to this person for you to devalue this person without knowing one thing about the person. Speaking of gossip, this is actually how gossip circulates in a manner that leads to the assassination of people's characters. We need only attach the word(s) to a person in order for it/them to stick. This is how mass media works as well. Through the tactful use of words, mainstream media has the power to literally make or break people. This is among the many reasons I've discontinued watching corporate news programming. When a person is attempting to free his/her mind, it grows increasingly tiring having thoughts and ideas inputted from corporate mediums. The mind remains forever captive when tethered to televisions. We have to limit our consumption of Eurocentric corporate media.

Let's zoom out a bit more. Imagine a scenario where a Black man is about to kill another Black man with a gun. In this instance, it is far easier for a Black man to murder a Black man if he sees him as just another nigger (or nigga). "Imma kill you nigga". ."I killed them niggas". .or "fuck them niggas" rolls off the tongue like bad movie lines and basic degenerate rap lyrics. Its world's easier to kill a man you view as just another "nigger". Now picture the same conflict scenario but replace the word nigga with "brotha", cousin, king, or family. From this vantage, it would seem far more difficult to end the life of someone you genuinely view in a positive light, someone you view as family. If we see one another as connected by blood, we're generally more inclined to employ far less harsh measures to resolve our conflicts. If psychologically, I've been trained and socialized to view all Black men as niggas, there's a much better chance that, without our actually knowing or acknowledging it, we view Black men collectively as possessing not much more value than what was bestowed upon us by racist slave masters who first assigned the word to us. We did not one day look up and have the word nigger as a term of endearment that projects brotherhood. We were socialized and suckered into its use. Now our children kill each other fueled by centuries of taught and learned self-hatred. We are not niggers or niggas, never have been. Europeans created the nigger as a major mentally debilitating illness. It took centuries for us to go from being proud Africans to embracing being American niggas. It'll take a while to wash it off.

What if the Black man saw Black women as sisters and queens and referred to them as often as possible with these titles? Would the misogyny that we've adopted from the larger Greco-Roman society be running amuck throughout our communities, our relationships, and our entertainment? If I am courting a woman I have been programmed to see as a "bitch", realistically, my respect for her has a built-in ceiling. The first few times we have a disagreement, she becomes the word I've been socialized to attach to all Black women. What is crazy is when we try to justify our use of the word on Black women we do not know. But not our own mothers and daughters. We will kill a NIGGA who disrespects our daughter by calling her a bitch. However, we are quick to target someone else's daughter with the same word, often followed by misogynistic actions. Bottom line is too many of us see ALL women as bitches. The only protection our women have is when they're some close kin of ours. The men of a community are tasked with the responsibility and obligation to protect the women of the community. When we help to define them as bitches for the world, we render them subject to disrespect from in and outside of the community. Who respects the men of a nation that don't demand respect for their women? I suspect our daughters would not grow to identify with boss and queen bitches if they KNEW that they were our African goddesses. Black men should nourish the self-esteem of the little Black girls around them instead of rendering our young daughters vulnerable to devaluation. No sister in the Black community ever birthed a bitch.

Honestly, the use of the n-word isn't an issue I soapbox a lot because I just stopped using the word about 7 years ago. It isn't a habit one can break overnight, especially when a person has been unconsciously using it about as much as blinking. I can honestly say that its discontinued usage has had a definite impact on how I view and interact with my people and our struggle. I do not enjoy hearing us calling each other these debasing terms. I understand we all have a way to go in realizing our true potential and eliminating barriers, both the physical and psychological variety. At the end of the day, I can't see where I'd be interested in any advocacy for the sake of liberating niggas and bitches. However, I am clear on who I struggle for and with.

(Proud Black people with raised Black Power salutes/source unknown)

CHAPTER 17
Connecting the Dots

Toxic propagandization aside, NWA was a musically talented rap group. But along with the negative imagery, there are ominous connections to conspiracies involving the group that cannot easily be dismissed as coincidence. A conspiracy is a secret plan to do something unlawful and harmful. Conspiracies against Black people by both Europeans and Jews is a lengthy list of savage injustices. Starting with that initial introduction on the west coast of Africa centuries ago, to an existence today that still finds us trying to convince others that we matter, Black lives have been saddled with the manifestations of constant conspiring. In ancient times, Greeks invaded Egypt stealing much of what they found, plagiarizing it, and submitting it as their own. The list of indiscretions against African people is lengthy and old enough to be scripted on papyrus.

When a people's culture is conquered, colonized, corrupted, and co-opted by another, it no longer serves that people's interests. It no longer serves as an enrichment tool for those who cultivated it. It becomes a mechanism of control that can be wielded by the conquerors against the conquered. Historically, we've seen this plenty. Hip Hop was not immune.

Crack Commanded

Crack cocaine was introduced to Black communities in L.A. in the 1980's. Crack is a crystallized form of cocaine made by cooking it with baking soda. Crack is smoked and is the most addictive way to ingest cocaine. It affects the brain a lot quicker, its more intense, and it generally features a high that only last about fifteen minutes. Crack addicts wind up spending entire days chasing after that next high. The thing that makes crack so attractive to drug addicts in impoverished Black communities is its affordability. Pure cocaine wasn't a drug those who were poor could afford. The creation of crack made cocaine accessible to the poor. The question rarely posed in relation to the influx of crack is, who was the enterprising Black cocaine dealer who one day decided to combine cocaine with baking powder to render it more accessible to poor Black communities? There is a precise method and a good amount of chemistry involved in the crack creation process. The general suspicion is that crack was a creation of the U.S. government, not some enterprising Black mad scientist in the 'hood. It's just one arsenal of weapons among many crafted to destabilize Black communities across America. The CIA and the FBI have been known and documented to have committed far worse atrocities against African people to fulfill racist agendas.

(Crack cocaine/Wikipedia.org, 2020)

Hip Hop, under its current ownership, is frequently used to promote negative images, narratives, and behaviors. It often glorifies the self-destructive, rendering it popular and something that should be embraced. The first reports of crack cocaine's use were in the early 1980's. It spread like a California wildfire, an immediate epidemic. It didn't take long for crack to take root in the Black communities of Los Angeles where it hit first. Like an atomic bomb, the devastation and the destruction were pervasive. People, families, marriages, and entire communities were and continue to be ravaged by the introduction of crack cocaine to Black communities. The crack epidemic eventually hit other major urban areas where Blacks were already struggling to survive America. The death tolls and arrests of young Blacks skyrocketed in concert with crack clamping down on areas where Blacks resided.

In 1987, NWA released its first single, *Panic Zone*. One of the b-sides on that release was *Dope Man*. *Dope Man* featured lyrics which promoted and glamorized the selling of crack cocaine.

"It was once said by a man who couldn't quit,

Dope man please can I have another hit.

The dope man said cluck I don't give a shit,

If your girl kneels down and sucks my dick.

It all happened, and the guy tried to choke her,

Nigga living in cash selling to smokers.

That's the way it goes, that's the way of the game,

Young brother getting over by slanging cane."

- Eazy E - NWA -

As mentioned earlier, Eazy E used money from drug dealing to fund NWA when they first formed the group. In L.A., at the same time Eazy E was dealing crack, "Freeway" Rick Ross was building his drug empire as a major coke distributor. As a youth in high school, Rick Ross was a star tennis player whose ambitions were cut short by the reality that is America's public schools for many young Black men. The schools hadn't taught him how to read. Tragically, it was a shop teacher who introduced Ross to the drug game. Ross grew as a cocaine supplier and began to expand his business rapidly. After a time, Ross connected with a Nicaraguan named Oscar Danilo Blandon who was a major Central American cocaine supplier. The Nicaraguan connect led to Ross becoming the main supplier of cocaine for both the Bloods and the Crips in L.A. Eazy E was a known Crip. Blandon's weighty deliveries also helped Ross expand his reach to become the supplier for Black communities in Kansas City, Oklahoma, Texas, St. Louis, Cincinnati, Cleveland, New Orleans, North Carolina, South Carolina, Baltimore, Seattle, Philadelphia, and New York. The song, *Dope Man*, served as an effective recruiting soundtrack for the drug game, much like the ubiquitous "be all you can be" army jingle still targeting America's impressionable young and poor, rendering imperialistic wars attractive. Most of NWA's music instructed Black youth to be much less than their potential with the same shared results, soldiers for the wrong side committing genocide.

Rick Ross's contact, Blandon, turned out to be the connection between the CIA and the Nicaraguan Contras in the well-documented Iran-Contra Affair. Much of this information came out as the result of interviews conducted by journalist Gary Webb where he spoke at length with Rick Ross and others involved. Gary Webb mysteriously wound up dead, shot in the head. Blandon was eventually hired by the U.S. Drug Enforcement Administration (DEA). This was probably a reward for his work helping the U.S. carry out its clandestine domestic and foreign policies. Domestically, the U.S. has always sought to maintain the subjugation of Blacks through the destabilization of Black families and communities. In foreign affairs, the U.S. has always possessed a level of expertise in destabilizing foreign governments, removing its leaders, and installing U.S. agents who act in the interests of America.

The Iran-Contra Affair took place during President Ronald Reagan's tenure in office. The affair featured the U.S. illegally selling arms to Iran in exchange for money which was used to fund the Nicaraguan Contras. The Contras were a group the U.S. financially supported to topple Nicaragua's Communist government at the time. Israel served as the middleman between the United States and Iran. Israel would provide a cover for U.S. malfeasance by providing the weapons, shipped to Israel from the United States, to Iran. Israel would then receive payment from the U.S. The way these transactions occurred concealed the fact that the U.S. was violating an embargo against Iran. The U.S. was supposedly selling arms to Iran in the hope Iran would free American hostages being held by a group associated with Iran. Oliver North of America's National Security Council was a major player. President Reagan claimed ignorance of anything beyond the coup employed to topple Nicaragua's communist government.

What was the connection between the Iran-Contra Affair and the drug trade in L.A.? Allegedly, the U.S. received tons of cocaine from Nicaraguan Contras. The U.S. used the proceeds from the sale of that cocaine in Black communities to help fund the Contra's efforts to overthrow the Communist Nicaraguan government.

(Time magazine cover, 1986)

The Iran-Contra Affair was just another sordid chapter in the Cold War between the U.S. and the Soviet Union. The U.S. has always had a major issue with Communism and has been willing to fund, initiate, and fight proxy wars to stop its existence and spread. The Red Scare run amuck. Capitalist countries can't colonize where Communism thrives. It's important that we study and understand both of these economic ideologies in order to understand much about the war-ridden world in which we live. In the years after WWII, millions of American soldiers and both soldiers and civilians on the Asian continent died in wars fought to stop Communism's spread. It boils down to economics, money. The U.S. government benefitted on two-fronts from the Iran-Contra affair. The U.S. was able to topple Nicaragua's Communist government while also setting Black progress in America back several decades through flooding Black communities with Central/South American cocaine. Despite numerous witness accounts to these transactions, including witnesses intimately involved, some who wound up dead, the U.S. denied culpability. Mission accomplished.

Eazy E was very likely connected to Rick Ross in order to receive drugs to sell. Rick Ross was a major cocaine distributor in L.A. Blandon supplied Ross. Blandon was the Nicaraguan link between the U.S. government and the Iran-Contra Affair. Eazy E went on to lend his voice to the promotion and glamorization of crack sells throughout America's Black communities with one of NWA's first releases, *Dope Man*. NWA provided the soundtrack for crack's proliferation throughout Black communities in the 1980's. In 1991, that picture grew a bit more ominous with Eazy E accepting an invitation to dine with George Bush Sr. at the White House. This happened only a year after Bush and the other Republican Conservatives had deemed his music obscene.

With President Bush

Only in America.

That was pretty much the reaction when hardcore rapper Eric "Easy-E" Wright of N.W.A. (Niggers With Attitude) fame was seen circulating amongst the GOP's (financial) nobility as a member of the National Republican Senatorial Committee Inner Circle during a recent invitation-only luncheon with the President.

Having claimed fame – or shame, depending on perspective – with such captivating tunes as "F--- tha Police," the self-described former drug dealer was unquestionably an enigma at the

Image from a Source article referring to Eazy E's Whitehouse visit during the presidency of President George H.W. Bush.(TheSource.com, Sha Be Allah, 2020)

Ronald Reagan was the President of the United States when NWA released the song, *Dope Man*. In 1982, President Ronald Reagan declared a War on Drugs. He eerily echoed the same declaration made by President Nixon in 1971. It was exposed by a Nixon Whitehouse aide, John Ehrlichman, that the War on Drugs declared by Nixon was enacted to harass and arrest Blacks and anti-Vietnam war protestors. Ehrlichman revealed that Nixon's War on Drugs had little to do with eradicating the scourge of drugs, but everything to do with containing and compromising Black movements and the anti-Vietnam protests being carried out by "hippies". In 1971, two of the U.S. government's biggest fears were Black progressive movements and the spread of Communism. The Vietnam War, which many "hippies" opposed, was fought to contain the spread of Communism, per President Truman's official Cold War policy of "containment". Ehrlichman commented on the Nixon policy's true intent:

"By getting the public to associate the hippies with marijuana and Blacks with heroin, and then criminalizing both heavily, we could disrupt those communities and vilify them night after night on the evening news"

Through his "war on drugs", Nixon was able to dissolve much of the anti-war movement along with whatever remnants of potent Black progressive movements that remained. Through propaganda campaigns connected to his War on Drugs, Nixon painted anyone who could in any way be associated with heroin and marijuana as criminals. Throughout the 1970's, Black communities were being plagued by the heroin epidemic. Most times jail was offered as a cure, not much prevention. Kid gloves are always applied with drug epidemics in White communities where the epidemics are treated as illnesses that require hospitalization and treatment. In Black communities, dealers, users, and the suspected are all herded into that criminal pool to be caged and painted as wicked. Somehow, America's crippling social policies always seem to escape that blame.

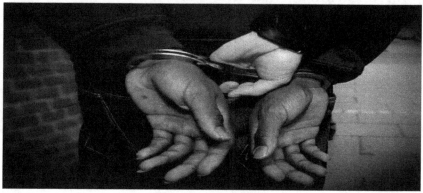

(Pinterest.com, 2020)

Fast forward to 1982 when President Reagan ramped up that same anti-Black Nixon fervor by declaring another "war on drugs". This time, the crack cocaine epidemic was the impetus behind the contrived criminalization campaign. A decade later with the exact same results, laws were passed, policies were changed, and law enforcement acted as frontline soldiers. In this war, thousands of Black people were corralled and incarcerated for dealing or possessing crack. The ulterior but obvious motive behind these efforts was the depopulation of urban areas. The rapidly blossoming prison industry had free and cheap labor demands to meet; Blacks were hired more than most to meet this need.

In 1994, Bill Clinton compounded efforts to fill America's prisons with Black people with his crime bill. Clinton's bill was known as the *Violent Crime Control and Law Enforcement Act of 1994*. Clinton, like his predecessors, used deceptive rhetoric to portray his bill as a means to end the scourge of drugs and the related violent crimes. His bill was later exposed to be just another policy employed to remove Black people from civilian life. His disingenuous admission and apology came about much later, after the damning effects of his bill. It was scarily effective. It had only a modest effect on actual crime rates, but Black incarceration rates increased exponentially.

Among its provisions were increased funding for tens of thousands of police officers and drug courts. It banned certain assault weapons and mandated life sentences for those convicted of a violent felony after two or more prior convictions, drug crimes included. The mandated life sentences became known as the "three-strikes" law. Clinton's crime bill also provided $8.7 billion to be spent towards erecting more prisons. America has always felt the inclination to fill prisons with as many Blacks as possible. Relatively paltry amounts of money were being directed towards the education of Black children. His bill included "truth-in-sentencing" laws which mandated that those convicted of violent crimes serve at least 85% of their sentences. Clinton incentivized states to build more prisons and to increase the sentences of the human beings housed in them. This directly contributed to the increased incarcerations of Black people. Clinton continued to target Black people in much the same was as his predecessors Nixon and Reagan.

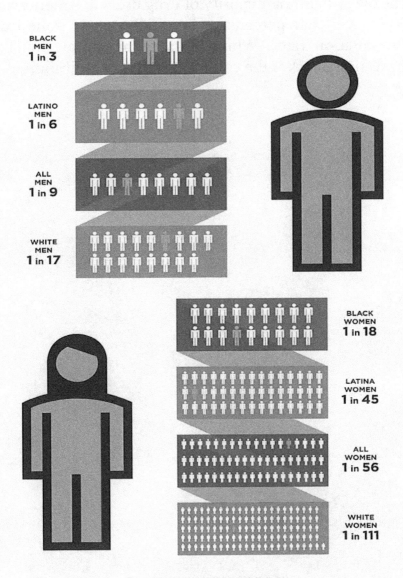

(TheSentencingProject.org, 2020)

Black people represent no more than around 12-14% of the total U.S. population of drug users but represent 59% of those in state prisons for drug offenses.

The overwhelming majority of drug users in America are White, yet that percentage isn't reflected in America's incarceration rates. White is the right complexion for protection. Black is the color targeted for eradication.

CHAPTER 18
The Bigger Picture

The status quo on planet earth sees a relatively small number of people controlling and consolidating the globe's abundant resources. The goal among this relatively small greedy minority is to maintain that control. It is not their intent to see the world's resources distributed in a way that sees those resources divided equally among the world's people. Wealth is consolidated into the hands of a few. The rest of the world fights for whatever is left after the hoarders have stolen far more than their fair share. The maintenance of this unbalanced distribution of wealth requires the use of covert and clandestine systems of control that lend to the subjugation and exploitation of the global majority. The best and easiest way to continue to manipulate and exploit people is through the control of the information they receive. Through the control of this information, people's thoughts, values, prejudices, beliefs, morals, and ethics are shaped. Desired behaviors and actions are obtained and maintained through this control. Through the manipulation of the world's mediums, media/information is utilized to distract or to remove attention away from critical issues while redirecting that attention to the inane, mundane, and trivial. We tend not to see the forest for the trees, tactfully placed foliage.

In America, most of the population has either accepted capitalism or doesn't totally understand how it works as America's driving economic system. Capitalism is America's modus operandi. As an economic system, it sees a small number of people living in extreme excess while around half the population is barely surviving. Being a check or two away from being destitute qualifies as barely surviving. Capitalism is cities where a relative few live in multimillion-dollar homes overshadowing streets where far too many find meals in garbage cans. Capitalism is humans as resources to be used, exploited, and disposed of when they are no longer profitable to company owners. It is state-provided schools that socialize students to accept debt and wage peonage as ways of life, a life of bi-weekly paychecks evidencing one's aptitude at earning the right to live. Ecosystems, animals, and the health of human beings come in far behind as priorities in comparison with the profit motive. Wars are initiated with the military industrial complex in mind. Laws are written in order to fuel the prison industrial complex where the continued enslavement of disenfranchised people helps bolster the GDP (gross domestic product). There is no humane or altruistic form of capitalism. Money is all that matters.

According to an early 2019 Washington Post article on America's wealth distribution, the top .00025% of the wealthiest Americans, 400 insanely rich people, own more of America's wealth than the 150,000,000 adult Americans that make up the bottom 60% of America's wealth distribution. Fifty percent of American households held 1.6% of America's wealth while the top 10% controlled 70% of that wealth. The richest country in the world is rife with an overwhelming majority who are impoverished. A handful of people in this country aren't willing to share so most don't eat their fair share.

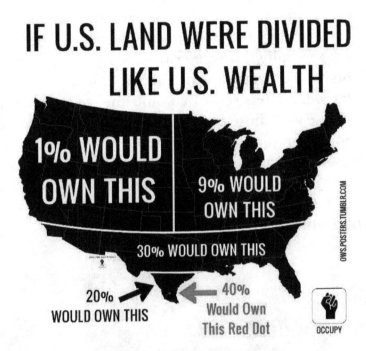

(OWSPosters.Tumblr.com, 2011)

Bread and Circuses

"Keeping the herd away from political issues allows them to pass bills overnight. Basically, they can go about ruining your life and bettering their own while you hope your favorite team gets a touchdown or worry about whether they'll make it into the playoffs or not. Another reason is consumerism. They can sell tickets to the sporting events, merchandise, food and beer etc. They can tier up your cable in a way so that you must pay a ridiculous amount of money per month to get all your sports channels. They fill the sporting events on TV with advertisements so the items will be imprinted in your brain next time you hit the stores."

-Brendan Bowes-

The philosophy of giving the masses "bread and circuses" isn't a new one. In Ancient Rome, the rulers constructed huge coliseums that hosted violent spectacles. They would pit men, generally slaves or criminals, against one another in fights to the death for the sake of entertainment. The winners were often rewarded, and the losers, well, they died. These grandiose events served the singular purpose of keeping the proletariat distracted while the emperors oppressed and ruled as they saw fit. The entertainment piece was just a by-product. By keeping people focused on games, the rulers could subject people to excessive taxation while amassing riches for themselves.

(Knowyourmeme.com, 2020)

As a bonus, the use of violent games dulled the human propensity towards compassion for other humans. Compassion and empathy for other human beings was viewed as a weakness in Ancient Rome. Socialized by these violent games, Roman citizens came to view violent wars as a means of maintaining Rome's self-professed "greatness". Men, women, and children were groomed into the acceptance and embracing of abject violence as a necessary component of governance. Does any of this sound familiar?

What has changed?

Today, all of America's media is controlled by 5 or 6 media giants. They decide what information reaches people and how and when it reaches them. Those who control media and control the government are one in the same. America has always been governed by the wealthy; in the past they were simply those who owned land. In many respects, this is still true. Today, America is what's been termed a "corporatocracy". It is a corporatocracy controlled by oligarchs. A corporatocracy is a society that is governed by very wealthy corporations, and oligarchs are wealthy corporate heads who wield a lot of political influence as a direct result of their wealth. Corporations and oligarchs directly influence voting and the passage of laws through political action committees (PACs) and interest groups/lobbyists. People are provided with the illusion of choices through elections and the constitutional right to vote, but very wealthy people get to set platforms and agendas which they ensure and enforce with money. They decide who and what qualifies for advocacy. Politicians, generally funneled to the American voters through one of two dominant parties, garner the majority of their financial support from corporations and are therefore more prone to enact legislation that benefits these corporations, the hands that feed them. America's democracy is a lengthy list of financial transactions. It is buyers and sellers. Metaphorically speaking, its pimps and hoes. Politicians serve as the hand puppets of the privileged while the poor get played. Regressive taxation exponentially increases the already heavy burden of those already saddled with debt and wage peonage.

The United States is the Roman Empire. We have become a society that has grown increasingly indifferent to militarism-fueled violence. The United States subjects marginalized people to abject violence both domestically and abroad. We concern ourselves with the imaginary, playing fantasy sports, while real war games increase human attrition, societal dysfunction, and the destruction and consolidation of the earth's resources.

The Machinery

A handful of mass media mediums make use of a multitude of distractive elements. Sports is just one element, just one tool in the arsenal that is the weaponry of those who command America's wealth. Through sports, we take in huge doses of pageantry and patriotism. Every sporting event sees us saluting an imperialism-saturated flag while saluting the soldiers who serve as the bagmen of an ever-expanding empire; colonialist crusaders.

Ever since Crispus Attucks and the American Revolution, Africans have been fighting for the right to fight in wars that have nothing to do with African people or African interests. America has never relented in the racist war being waged against Black people. I have yet to witness the battalion of soldiers protecting the interests of Black people. That sort of patriotism is forbidden. Rest well Fred

Hampton and the long list of others who America killed for daring to value Black lives.

Today, Africans are happily recruited by the United States in the interests of maintaining a sizable military, a military with around 800 bases worldwide. Oftentimes, joining the military is the only option many Blacks have due to societal barriers such as poverty, substandard schools, and unemployment. Every televised and attended sporting event in America, we're continuously sold the idea that we should be happy to go kill people for a country that loves us in last place. Poor people all across America are subjected to the same.

Sport dulls our senses to the idea of men owning men for the sake of entertaining the masses. The entertainment value of sports has rendered the Roman Coliseum delicious. Debilitating violence as entertainment is palatable and easy to consume. We love the violent nature of the games that feature the maimed, concussions, and retirees dying prematurely from head trauma. Much like in Ancient Rome, we've come to view the gladiators as heroes we should worship for their athleticism.

The compensation bestowed upon many of America's Black athletes often infects them with an arrested development many of our similarly well-compensated and elevated are stricken with. This arrested development prevents them from utilizing the money their owners pay them to build within the communities they matriculate from. Many of our athletes, through American media and subpar schooling, are taught only to enrich others. Turkeys and gym shoes around Thanksgiving and children's Christmas gifts suffice as community support.

At most, some Black athletes have opened charter schools for Black children that host Euro-centered curricula. In too many cases, the athletes are just the faces of these schools, no involvement beyond the connections to the education companies opening these privatized and profitable schools. I've never understood why a group of athletes don't band together to create and finance their own corporate franchises versus buying into ones owned by others. A small pool of Black millionaires can accomplish a lot for their own communities, the impactful and the sustainable. To be fair, a few athletes are actually going this route, but most simply don't know any better. America's schools breed self-centered capitalists, not citizens who embrace the communal. The athletes who dedicate themselves to the sort of advocacy our communities thirst for are the exception. The Black person who is willing to exploit his own people for a paycheck is a manifestation of an American education.

Fear prevents many of our best and brightest from using their lofty platforms and voices to address the societal issues that directly affect the people who look like them a few class rungs below on that caste ladder. Many of today's athletes are unable to engage in any meaningful advocacy because they are the victims of a system that has exploited them financially since they were teenagers. A system which values their athletic prowess. They are racehorses with more pronounced personalities. High school prepares stellar athletes to be exploited by the NCAA. The NCAA prepares our elite athletes to be exploited by professional sports. I'm looking forward to seeing our athletes break free from professional plantations and create their own professional leagues. Until then, we need to somehow make it attractive for our pro-bound athletes to become real heroes in their respective communities, not just on TV.

Sports is a multi-billion-dollar industry in America and the athletes only see a paltry sum of those immense profits compared to the Roman emperors and senators who man the owner's boxes overlooking the arenas. The owners of these teams are quite content with this arrangement. Players are just game pieces to be profited from and owners are quick to part with these pieces when they negatively affect profits. It's all business, but any business that doesn't allow a Black man or woman to meaningfully advocate for their own communities is a plantation. It's an oppressive institution where standing with a straightened back could get one punished, whipped. Sports as entertainment in America far surpasses community advocacy and activism as a priority. This hierarchy is impressed upon its employees. A functionally dysfunctional society requires this. Much of the little free time most people are allotted in this capitalist experiment is dedicated to watching and cheering on gladiators in arenas and on television. Simultaneously, our minds are being trained to cheer on the gladiators America sends to other countries to kill and maim for the sake of expanding and preserving America's way of being. Please stand for the pledge.

Reality is, the Black athlete is an extension of the Black collective and we're all manifestations of this system we struggle within. If we aren't educating our Black athletes and preparing them to become community leaders, we are allowing others to do so in their own interests. Much like many of us, they are socialized to serve the empire. Many of us, through our public and private employment, are serving the same. Most of our consumption habits reflect our complicity in America's agenda to assimilate and integrate us. We've embraced American culture at the expense of our own culture. We have cosigned our own *Dawes Act.* This disease of disconnectedness doesn't just affect our athletes, we're all afflicted. We can only cure ourselves through the realization that we are indeed ill. We have to release our minds, free them. The dominant society will never place the emancipation of our Black minds on that "things to do" list. That initiative is on us. We all need leisure time and relaxation. Part of that is unplugging and allowing ourselves to be entertained. But is it feasible for those having war waged against them daily to spend the majority of their time immersed in diversions from reality? The purpose of entertainment is to temporarily distract us from that reality, not replace it. In addition, the staged pageantry in much of America's entertainment melts our minds into a mainstream that's both complicit in and accepting of America's militarism. Extreme moderation is necessary.

Mainstream media compels us to celebrate rich people. In addition to gladiator worship, America hosts a Hollywood culture that creates overnight stars, people we look up to. We look up to them because the media places these otherwise regular human beings on pedestals for us to gaze upwards. The affixed fame and the attached fortunes that come party to "rising above the rest" are what we've been taught to applaud. What they do and say commands much of our attention. Many of our artists are very talented and definitely worthy of our accolades, but not our worship. Oftentimes, we're so blinded stargazing that we ignore any and all indiscretions these stars may have enacted against our community. We refuse to hold them accountable because of their fame. No community thrives with the inability or unwillingness to hold its own accountable for actions against the collective. America's media leads many of us to render certain human beings infallible, unable to do wrong. Most of these famous people exploit our blind loyalty, amass wealth at our expense, and never find cause to contribute anything meaningful to the Black community. We need to cultivate a collective self-love where we support those who support us. If they only see value in other people and their own popularity, allow them to go and be among those who make them happy. Race-traitors should never feel comfortable among us regardless of their appeal to our emotions. Most men or women would eventually part ways with a spouse who operates against the interests of the relationship or family. The same applies. We can't continue as doormats.

When we adjust our eyes and look upon things as they should be seen, we understand that within America, rewards are reaped upon those who have the most value to the owners within the system. Many times, talent has little to do with it, unless one considers contrived popularity a talent. Or unless one considers the ability or willingness to be a weapon used against us a talent. In Hollywood, many Black artists are often employed in this manner. Many of the scripts and narratives they adhere to more than often cast the African collective as very simple one-dimensional people. This is the nature of our existence here, but when does it end? I applaud all Black entertainers who have defied the owners of these platforms and refused to commit to work that debases Black people. I salute them. Commentary on our dysfunction is the fact that we are more prone to applaud rich race traitors than we are to applaud those who have sacrificed on our behalf and been punished for it. Again, America's media determines who our heroes are.

It is disturbing to think about the number of Black athletes who have been and continue to be exploited by the NCAA (National Collegiate Athletic Association), NBA (National Basketball Association), and the NFL (National Football League). If Black athletes walked away from either of these platforms, these leagues would shut down overnight, billion-dollar industries. We haven't used that leverage and we continue to settle. Much respect to Colin Kaepernick and the few others who "get it", but it's tragic when one man has the courage to make a statement in support for African people being gunned down by police officers, and most Black athletes are afraid to stand with him. Talk about being left "hanging". Interestingly enough, the media has so much power over many of us that Colin's stand and continuing exile from the NFL has just about been forgotten by many NFL players who have ignored his courageous gesture and continue to play. Throngs of Black NFL fans continue to support, full fervor. Guess I can't blame the other Black athletes for not sacrificing as Colin did. It appears unlikely that as a collective, we'd have their backs. We don't own the NFL, but it appears to own many of us. Being entertained is the priority, not being people of pride and integrity. Much respect to NFL baller, Eric Reid, who continues to have Kaep's back, utilizing his platform to advocate for Black people.

Historically, we've seen many Black athletes and actors punished, dethroned, and blacklisted for simply trying to advocate for Black people. There are plenty who've tried.

Within the constructs that are American sports and Hollywood, real advocacy and activism for the sake of Black people is generally frowned upon, its cause for dismissal. The many instances of Blacks using their voices to address Black concerns and being "blacklisted" for it magnifies the need Black people to own and control our own leagues and media. Much respect to Paul Robeson, Eartha Kitt, Danny Glover, Jessie Williams, Muhammad Ali, Craig Hodges, Mahmoud Abdul-Rauf, Colin Kaepernick and many others who spoke up and had their pockets taxed. Much love to those in that vein I have not listed.

Colin Kaepernick (Mike McCarn/AP File, 2016)

We must begin to see our athletes/entertainers and the actual value they possess versus the assigned value attached to them by their owners. Actually, the same applies across the spectrum, in every way we're employed as Black people in this country. We need to begin to see value in those Black athletes and entertainers who see value in the Black communities they come from. Again, the same goes for the Black teacher, police officer, banker, or corporate CEO. Do they actually have value to us or is the fame or fortune bestowed upon them solely as a result of their value to other races of people? The Black athlete and entertainer who make millions through their employment in the NBA or in Hollywood makes those millions because they possess talents that help enrich their owners, they are profitable.

All of us need to find ways to return value to our respective communities that mirrors whatever success we have garnered within America. We have to eventually adopt a mindset that sees us not solely celebrating Blacks based on this exported value, exported gifts and talents. What internal value do they possess? Are these entertainers utilizing their gifts and talents in a way that helps the Black community, or are they just tools of wealthy Whites? Yes, we all have to eat, and most of us are employed in varying capacities by people who don't look like us. Are we sharing our value with our own or are we just prostituting ourselves out to others and then taking that compensation and consuming in a manner that only enriches others? Bottom line is we have to begin to truly hold ourselves accountable to us. If a Black person has earned over a billion dollars working for others but has not given back to the Black community in any meaningful, sustainable way, they do not have any real value to us. What good is their ability to entertain us? Are they employed to make us feeling good about being in last?

We live in a system that rewards Black people who are apolitical and asocial while severely punishing those who put in work for us. The Black luminary who pushes a status quo agenda is among the most rewarded among Blacks. We have had hundreds of Black celebrities who were paid millions and have had monuments erected in their honor by their employers. We have watched many of our greatest Black heroes, people who have dedicated their lives to us, die poor with little beyond what they wore. And that is if they were not simply censored via assassination. Most times, the media has guided us towards derision of our real heroes. We've become a people who celebrate men who dunk basketballs exponentially more than we appreciate those who fight for us through community-rooted activism. We will defend the toxic rapper who is treated unfairly by America's justice system before we lift our voices for those pro-Black Africans we have wasting away in America's jails for decades, locked up for being pro-Black. This is a direct manifestation of not owning our own media, owning ourselves. We are directed to celebrate those who operate against our collective health while ignoring or directing ire towards those who fight for our freedom. Ignorance is celebrated while the Black intellect is often ostracized and eviscerated. We do not possess the media control to display and promote who and what we should. However, while we possess the resources to, we do not direct our monies towards the entities, institutions, or individuals that we should. We gift our vast community resources to what is promoted by those who already own the mediums. This enables them to continue to promote their interests over our own.

CHAPTER 19
Out of Sight, Out of Mind

America's media doesn't promote the fact that America and Europe became extremely wealthy through conquering, colonizing, and economically exploiting places around the world where people of color reside. Africa has felt most of this pain. It is not a picture America's wealthiest 1% would like us to focus our attention on. Frequently, we get to hear about how great America is though. We get to hear about how rich America is. Not many of us question how America became so "great" and so extraordinarily rich. In 1884, there was a conference held in Berlin, Germany where European nations carved up Africa for the purpose of colonization. European countries allocated Africa's vast resources among themselves, no African consent. This is how the United States and its allies became "great"

Africa is easily the most abundant continent on the planet resource-wise. It's huge in terms of land mass and its location and various tropical and temperate climates lend to its resource abundance. Sadly enough, Africa is the poorest continent on the planet in terms of its share of the planet's fiat currency. Despite the fact that it's the richest resource-wise, its poor. Africa is only poor because it's been robbed and continues to be robbed. The biggest thieves are America and its European allies. Historically, they have proven to be Africa's greatest antagonists. Black people in America rarely get a peek into the actual economic exploitation being reaped upon Africa. We've been taught to patriotically accept America's top position and to embrace the means America advanced in order to achieve that position. Lots of plundering, lots of murder, lots of rape, and a whole lot of imperialism.

The African continent is impoverished by the efforts of America and its European allies, mass militarism. The same Africans who were kidnapped and exported to America as part of Africa's centuries long exploitation of Africa now celebrate the exact militarism that continues to exploit Africans in America and on their home continent. America has created the African who wants to "be all he can be" at the expense of his/her own global majority, African people. Black self-hatred goes psychologically far deeper than what most of us truly understand or are willing to contend with. This "New African" is the invention of American media, the same way the "nigger" is. Information that would empower African people in America is rarely, if ever, distributed through America's mass corporate media. The revolutionary will not be televised.

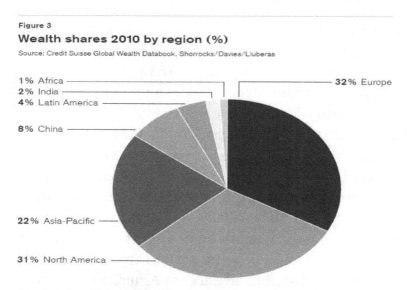

Figure 3
Wealth shares 2010 by region (%)
Source: Credit Suisse Global Wealth Databook, Shorrocks/Davies/Lluberas

1% Africa
2% India
4% Latin America
8% China
32% Europe
22% Asia-Pacific
31% North America

(Credit Suisse Global Wealth Databook, Sherrocks/Davies/Liuberas, 2010)

CHAPTER 20
World War Propaganda

"The propagandist's purpose is to make one set of people forget that certain other sets of people are human"

- Aldous Huxley -

The major purpose of America's media machinery is as a conduit for the distribution of propaganda. Propaganda is disseminated through television, radio, movies, the internet, newspapers, and magazines. It often comes disguised as what we are either informed by or entertained with. It usually enters our minds as that Trojan horse I mentioned previously. On the surface, most entertainment or televised news is presented as something beneficial, but in actuality, these media gifts conceal covert, intentional, and very functional efforts to sway. The use of propaganda is deceitful in nature. The goal is to help shape our thoughts and ideas at the expense of our own inward critical thoughts, analysis, and self-cultivated positions. What makes propaganda deceptive is our not realizing our thoughts and ideas are being shaped. Generally, the propagandist is seeking to craft thoughts and ideas that support their own agendas or interests.

The U.S. military is among the biggest purveyors of propaganda in America. Among their goals is to propagate a populace who not only will send their children into combat in foreign countries, but also a population that will support, promote, and celebrate America's militarism. Americans are a lot easier to govern when all, regardless of race, creed, or culture, buy into the European's centuries ago conceived concept of Manifest Destiny, their divine right to rule. With their gods, they've conquered. In their gods, we've trusted.

Propaganda is often used to shape ideas and thoughts as they apply to certain groups of people. It can be used to glamorize certain groups while dehumanizing others. Those who control the dissemination of propaganda to the masses typically depict themselves in ways that, overall, portray themselves in a positive light. It's the people who are the targets of exploitation and subjugation in a society who wind up the victims of that society's negative propaganda. The victims are portrayed in ways that render their exploitation, subjugation, and even elimination acceptable to the general public. There's no large-scale outcry when the negatively propagandized are eventually euthanized.

The Use of Propaganda During WWII

"Make the lie big, make it simple, keep saying it, and eventually they will believe it"

- Adolph Hitler -

During the 1930's, in the years leading up to World War II, the Nazis mounted propaganda campaigns to demonize and dehumanize the Jews living in Germany. Hitler appointed his close friend, Joseph Goebbels, as the head of the Nazi's Ministry of Public Enlightenment and Propaganda. Goebbels orchestrated and implemented massive propaganda campaigns using the radio, posters, and motion pictures to depict Jews as the people of

Germany who possessed no value, and therefore, weren't worthy of life.

Goebbels's pieced together a propaganda campaign that set to reinforce certain despicable stereotypes about Jewish people. His campaign portrayed Jews as materialistic, untrustworthy, physically unattractive, and rootless wanderers. As part of this campaign, German women were warned against sex with Jewish men. Does this sound familiar yet?

Hitler issued what were known as the *Nuremberg Race Laws of 1935*. Under these laws, Jews were excluded from holding many high-profile jobs. They were locked out of public office, teaching, farming, radio, theatre, and film. Gradually, they were stripped of the right to practice law and medicine. They also were eventually banned from public places throughout Germany. Under these laws, marriage and relationships with Jews were prohibited. Jews were forbidden from entering most stores. Stores were forbidden from selling necessities like food or pharmaceuticals to them. It was a Hitler-enforced Jim Crow for Jews.

In 1941, after six years of targeting Jews with the most debasing propaganda, Hitler began what came to be known as Hitler's "Final Solution". With the stage set and hostile climate crafted by Goebbel's campaign, Hitler initiated the final chapter of his Jewish persecution with the expressed goal of exterminating all Jews from Germany. From 1941-1945, Jews were shot, medically experimented on, set on fire, or marched into chambers filled with poisonous gas to be executed. Many were starved to death awaiting these fates. There were many in

Germany at the time who saw the mistreatment of the Jews as warranted which is why it continued on such a massive scale for four years unabated. Goebbels had done his job well as the Nazi propaganda chief. When a people are largely viewed as less than human in the eyes of the dominant society, their murders are easier to stomach.

Top: Adolf Hitler and his Minister of Propaganda, Joseph Goebbels. (Amp.dw.com, 2017). Bottom: Crematoria where the bodies of Jews were cremated after the Nazi's mass murders by carbon dioxide gas poisoning. (Encyclopedia.ushmm.org, 2018)

To help with the dissemination of Nazi propaganda during World War II, the Nazis had hired Bertlesmann Publishing. The head of Bertlesmann at the time was Heinrich Moen. Bertlesmann published a variety of anti-Jewish papers and books to assist the Nazi war effort. Bertlesmann published material that was distributed to German youth that defamed, degraded, and dehumanized Jews. It was also found that Bertlesmann made use of Jewish slave labor at his publishing facilities outside of Germany. Bertlesmann Publishing claimed to have never been an organization within the Nazi Party, but its association with Nazi efforts is clear. During the Nazi campaign in Germany, Bertlesmann published and printed 19 million books making it the largest publisher for the German army. The company shut down its publishing in Germany in 1944 with the Allied Powers advancing on Germany. They attempted to evaporate their ominous ties to the Nazis.

Bertlesmann concealed its work with the Nazi party for years. This enabled Bertlesmann to be issued a new license to publish books in the years following WWII. Bertlesmann returned to its roots as a major publisher of school textbooks. In 2013, Bertlesmann joined with Pearson publishing to combine their worldwide distribution. With that merger, Bertlesmann and Pearson came to control Random House/Penguin Publishing, giving it a (25%) share of the world's publishing business. The Bertlesmann company also has substantial influence within the music industry in Europe and in the United States. It's no wonder so much toxic anti-Black propaganda has been infused into the Black music distributed by these global conglomerates. It also doesn't come as a surprise when a publishing giant such as McGraw-Hill can distribute schoolbooks in Texas that portray centuries of forced servitude in the Americas as a "voluntary arrangement" between Europeans and Africans instead of the forced and deadly servitude it was in reality. There's no better way to alleviate the guilt or the need for slavery reparations than to gradually erase America's anti-Black indiscretions from history. Media control allows these conglomerates to not only distort and redefine images and narratives, it also grants them the power to rewrite history.

Without a doubt, most Jews understand clearly the negative impact a targeted propaganda campaign can have on a group of vulnerable citizenry given their own not long ago history. They also understand the importance of protecting and empowering the minds of Jewish children. It's ironic that so many Jews manipulate and control an entertainment industry that sees the masses of African people all over the globe the subjects of one of the most insidious propaganda campaigns ever mounted against a group of people.

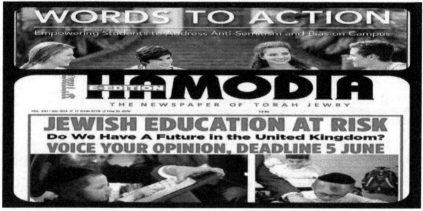

Top: Words to Action is a "training program to empower and equip college students with constructive and effective responses to combat anti-Semitism and anti-Israel bias on campus". Bottom: Hamodia consists of "in-depth news for Israel and the Jewish community; politics, editorials, terrorism, technology, Jewish culture and community". This issue is focused on Jewish education in the United Kingdom.

CHAPTER 21
Who Stole the Soul?

Hip Hop was initially seen as a fad by the establishment. It was expected to fizzle out after a few years. It wasn't respected as an artform by those outside of the environment and climate that birthed it. Today, Hip Hop is a giant. Hip Hop is infused into just about every aspect of our existence. Who would of thought way back at the beginning that Hip Hop would be utilized in just about every other commercial on television today? Hip Hop is the most co-opted and misappropriated. Just about every race and culture on the planet has adopted Hip Hop in some form and infused it with its own local vibe. Hip Hop artists have garnered world fame and even the older artists are still making money touring. Once it was realized that Hip Hop was going to be the gift to America that just kept giving, huge corporations and global conglomerates wanted their piece.

The global expansion of Hip Hop was both a gift and a curse. It's beautiful to see this art form that was created by ingenious kids from the Bronx projects become something that would grow to become a global phenomenon. The unfortunate part about that growth is that as Hip Hop grabbed the attention of the world, those who could, sought to own it. As with just about everything that emanates from the minds of African people, it was stolen by others and utilized in a manner that garnered tremendous wealth for capitalistic thieves while the originators were left to pocket whatever they could through crooked contracts and conniving conspirers. The face of Hip Hop is no longer that of the kids who understood and embraced Hip Hop's foundational elements. Hip Hop's new face is people and companies that weren't around when it was conceived.

The control of media around the world is in the hands of a relative few. This means that the flow of information around the world is filtered and manipulated by a handful of people. The same applies with music. These giant companies get to decide what artists get signed, promoted, and paid well. These companies also decide what messages get promoted throughout the music they distribute. The new industry dynamic that sees Black artists owned by Jews and Whites has created some real conflicts of interests. Many of Hip Hop's new landlords manage investment portfolios that influence both rap culture and prison policy.

The new owners of Hip Hop tend to be international investment firms that have no connection to Hip Hop beyond the companies they control. For them, the culture is just a commodity. Investment firms are only interested in making money. They have no vested interest in Hip Hop or the people who love it. Hip Hop is just another culture to be co-opted, convoluted, and profited from. As parasites do, when there's no more life left to be extracted from an artform, they are on to the next cultural creation to commercialize it.

Globally, Hip Hop is a multi-billion-dollar industry. The prison industry in the United States enjoys this distinction as well. No other country incarcerates more of its citizens than the United States of America. Proportionally, most of the people locked up are America's most disenfranchised population, Black people. Blacks are no more than 13-14%

of the U.S. population, but somehow make up around 35% of those incarcerated. One would have to assume that either Black people are innately criminal or that there's a sinister system set up to railroad Blacks into prisons. The latter conclusion can be easily proven via the historical, quantitative, and volumes of the qualitative. The deck is stacked against us. Only the devout racist or profoundly ignorant individual would accept some moral deficiency as cause for the horrific numbers of incarcerated Black men and women.

"Arguably the most important parallel between mass incarceration and Jim Crow is that both have served to define the meaning and significance of race in America. Indeed, a primary function of any racial caste system is to define the meaning of race in its time. Slavery defined what it meant to be black (a slave), and Jim Crow defined what it meant to be black (a second-class citizen). Today mass incarceration defines the meaning of blackness in America: black people, especially black men, are criminals. That is what it means to be black."

- Michelle Alexander –

Black people continue to be criminalized and imprisoned for reasons both social and economic. Locking people up is a means of control but it's also a major means of making money. America's brand of capitalism calls for it. The most subjugated are cast as the most exploited, our role in America since we've been here. The economic exploitation of certain groups of people is the wind that that fills capitalist sails. Incarcerating Black people en masse is profitable because prisons employ people in small rural towns starved for employment. The local prison's inmates are counted towards the census which helps these small towns to snare federal funding. Criminal justice systems within municipalities make money processing the criminalized, arrested, and prosecuted from among the poor.

Prisons contract outside companies for a variety of facility needs. There are phone companies that prisons contract to enable prisoners to place calls to friends and family on the outside. Prisons contract food and food preparation, furniture, prison uniforms, and even the medical care of prisoners. All of these entities are profit driven.

Optimal exploitation of America's prisoners sees them manufacturing items for department stores and industries looking to cut costs. Per the 13th amendment, prisoners can be exploited for free labor. Anyone convicted of a crime and incarcerated qualifies. Prisons are being built in rural towns at a much higher clip than schools are being erected in poor urban communities. The goal isn't the eradication of poverty as prevention, but the criminalization of the poor to feed the blossoming prison industry, bolstering America's already over-inflated GDP.

Recently, states and the federal government have been turning over its prisons to private entities, prisons for profit. Imagine if you're one of these investment firms and your portfolio includes both Hip Hop music and private prisons. Both are immensely profitable but imagine being able to manipulate one to feed the other.

Since the end of the 1980's, the paradigm in Hip Hop had begun to shift. Hip Hop's mainstream went from featuring rap that inspired and empowered Black kids to music that debased and criminalized Black children. There wasn't a demand for disrespectful, misogynistic music from consumers of Hip Hop, it just suddenly became what was featured, paid for, and promoted. Artists like Public Enemy and Brand Nubian were forced underground. The landscape changed. Hip Hop had new owners and those owners were looking for ways to profit from what they valued as a commodity, not a vibrant culture. What if the impressionable minds of Black children could be impacted in a way that lent to criminal behavior helping to fill prison beds, beds in prisons owned and operated by the same owners of Hip Hop? What if there was money to be made by keeping private prison beds occupied? What if 9/10 of the Hip Hop songs played on urban radio featured music where Black boys are promoting the senseless shootings of other Black men? What if the Black boys and girls in most of the music identified with being self-labeled niggers and bitches? What if many of the Black male artists bragged about drugging and raping Black women throughout their songs? What if abject ignorance and ignorant behavior were promoted to Black children as cool while lyricism and intelligence were demoted to something that no longer mattered? What if just about every song promoted rampant drug and alcohol use? What if most of the music filled the minds of Black youth with materialism with drug peddling as a tangible means to acquire over-priced wants? Would these prisons fill up a lot faster if Black children began to see no value in themselves?

Of course, they would.

Shortsightedness would lend to one declaring that negative media (Gangster Rap, Reality TV, violent Hollywood movies, etc.) are solely responsible for the negative, wayward behaviors that land many of our children in prisons, or worse, in morgue drawers. No way. It's much deeper, but we better believe the poisoning of the minds and spirits of Black children through toxic media plays a major role. Its basic science. Music has always been the most formidable way of transmitting a people's culture. Today, what has been defaced and rebranded as Black culture is rife with negative imagery and portrayals. It is no wonder many of our children under-value their own lives and often see no value in the lives of those who look like them. Combine this psychological warfare with the economic, social, and academic beat downs our children are already contending with and we get the recipe for an entire generation of disconnected and disenchanted children who have been primed for this burgeoning prison industry. We can't ever dismiss the role negative propaganda plays in our oppression. We can't dismiss it as a component of Black genocide. Remember, a masterfully degrading propaganda campaign preceded Hitler's attempt to erase Jews from the planet.

Untangling That Web

". .it was about media powers seeking out the biggest pretend criminal kingpins they can find, (many of whom who shamelessly adopt the names of actual real-life criminal kingpins like 50 Cent and Rick Ross) and exalting them as the poster children for a culture. It was about an art form reduced to product placement, the selling of a lifestyle, and ultimately, a huge ad for imprisonment. ."

- Homeboy Sandman (Rap Rehab) –

The exact same people who own American media, including mediums that feature Hip Hop, are the exact same people who own privatized prisons. The owners of these huge investment portfolios that include both Hip Hop and private prisons have plenty of motivation to use one institution to pad the profits of the other; the profit motive. These venture capitalists have the means to utilize the degradation of Hip Hop to fill private prisons. What else would justify such an abrupt paradigm shift? Again, Black youth never demanded more negative Hip Hop, it's what's been offered as the only alternative.

1. BAIN CAPITAL is a huge investment/private equity firm founded by both Mitt Romney and Bill Bain. BAIN CAPITAL owns iHEART COMMUNICATIONS.

2. BAIN CAPITAL also owns a significant stake in privatized prisons.

3. iHEART COMMUNICATIONS owns WGCI, Chicago's urban radio station and Hot 97, NYC's largest urban station. (Emmis Communications is the direct owner of Hot 97 but, as of 2012, fell under the media umbrella that is iHeart Communications)

4. CCA (CORRECTIONS CORPORATION OF AMERICA) is among the companies owned and managed by BAIN CAPITAL.

5. CCA owns and manages private prisons and detention centers.

6. The largest holder of CCA is VANGUARD GROUP INC. (VANGUARD is an investment management group with $3 trillion in assets).

7. VANGUARD is the 3rd largest holder of VIACOM and TIME-WARNER (TIME-WARNER owns New Line Cinema, HBO, CNN, Cartoon Network, CBS/Warner Brothers Television (CW), and DC Comics).

8. VIACOM owns BET and MTV.

9. VANGUARD is the 3rd largest holder of the GEO GROUP.

10. GEO GROUP is a company that manages correction, detention, and community re-entry centers.

11. GEO GROUP is 2nd only to CCA in regard to correction, detention, and community re-entry centers.

12. GEO is located in the U.S., the United Kingdom, Australia, and South America.

13. BLACKROCK INC. is the world's largest asset manager.

14. BLACKROCK INC. is the #1 holder of VIACOM and TIME WARNER.

15. BLACKROCK is the 2nd largest holder of CCA.

16. BLACKROCK is the 6th largest holder of the GEO group.

*Note: New media mergers, consolidations, and acquisitions occur quite frequently so these media relationships may have changed since this book was first conceived. The overall dynamic remains the same.

Money Decides Legislation

The investment firms that control all media and the private prison industry have more than enough money to get things done on Capitol Hill. Lobbyists in Washington D.C. serve as extensions of these investment firms. They are the foot soldiers that help these companies maintain their foothold in the industries they manipulate. Regulation of these industries is stifled through lobbying. They control the game and they set the rules with money. Lobbyists are individuals hired by corporations to influence decisions made by government officials, usually lawmakers or members of regulatory agencies. These large corporations pay lawyers to go to Congress to influence lawmakers to pass laws that help pad their pockets. Cash rules everything.

Money helps rich racists control the lives of the poor. The American Legislative Exchange Council is a nonprofit organization of conservative lawmakers and representatives of the private sector who help draft legislation (make laws) in both the federal and state governments. ALEC is funded by both the Corrections Corporation of America and the GEO group, both groups that build and profit from profit prisons. Through the funding of ALEC, these companies make certain that laws and policies are promoted that help them to profit from their holdings. They successfully championed the incarceration-promoting "truth-in-sentencing" and "three-strike" laws that significantly increased the numbers of Black people locked away in prisons. Bill Clinton was the President who signed these bills into laws. The largest rise in incarcerations coincides with early 80's prison privatizations despite overall crime actually declining. Remember, both crack and NWA's dope-slangin' sonnets flooded Black communities at the same time incarceration rates climbed; talk about the perfect storm. The majority of those locked up were Blacks and Latinos for drug arrests. Both Black and Latino kids are encouraged plenty to partake in and peddle drugs through music prison owners profit from.

Corporate Complicity

The United States has laws that prohibit the importation of goods manufactured using prison or child labor. The *Tariff Act of 1930* prohibits the importation of merchandise produced, in whole or part, by prison labor slaves, or the forced labor of children. Of course, enforcing this law for compliance often proves difficult as the U.S. has only limited access to policing entities in other countries. Plenty of companies that sell goods in America have been exposed and found to be contracting entities that employ both the labor of prisoners and children. The law is difficult to enforce and with such a profit-driven economic system like capitalism, companies have plenty of incentive to dismiss the humanity of people in lieu of those profits. Greed more than often supersedes the good intentions of altruistic laws.

The U.S. is often the epitome of hypocrisy. The U.S. frowns upon the use of prison and child labor by other countries but employs the same within its own borders. The 13th Amendment supposedly abolished slavery but upon closer inspection, there is a built-in exception. Slavery is illegal until one is convicted of a crime and incarcerated. Once a person is incarcerated, they can be enslaved. What a twist. In order for America to ensure a good number of Africans could still be forced to work for free, it simply locked more of them away in prisons. Blacks are incarcerated disproportionately more than Whites; exponentially more. Laws and the way most Blacks are forced to live in this country ensures this. The New Jim Crow is Mass Incarceration.

Capitalism provides corporations with plenty of incentive to overlook the human rights of certain groups of people. Immigrants, the disenfranchised, and the poor in America are exploited plenty for their labor by companies hell bent on cutting corners and saving money. Some people are underpaid in cash and prisoners are basically paid pennies, if anything. Among the more ridiculous aspects of prison labor is the fact that Black unemployment has historically remained high in America. Meanwhile, work that could be distributed among unionized and protected Black laborers outside of prisons is being performed for almost free by imprisoned Black men. For these greedy corporations, it's about maintaining their ledgers in the black on the backs of Blacks.

Some of America's biggest and most popular corporations have saved a few coins employing the incarcerated. Victoria's Secret, Johnson and Johnson, Wal-Mart, McDonald's, Wendy's, Sara Lee, United Airlines, Verizon, AT&T, Sprint, Fruit of the Loom, Mary Kay Cosmetics, JP

Morgan and Company, Allstate Insurance, Proctor and Gamble, Microsoft, and a host of others utilize prison labor to manufacture their goods or to perform services. The plantations in America never closed shop and they remain populated by the exact same people, those who were kidnapped and coerced into building this country. You best believe some of the same corporations that own media and prisons also own some of the above listed companies. Again, they can easily use portions of their investment portfolios to pad the profits of the others; devilish diversification.

"Made me reflect on a time when we were 3/5th of them,

Chains and powerless,

Brave souls reduced to cowardice. . .

Rich White man rule the nation still,

Only difference is we all slaves now,

The chains concealed."

- J. Cole -

WAR

The "wars on drugs" waged under Nixon and Reagan were waged entirely in low income communities of color. The United States government appears to have helped flood Black communities with crack cocaine and then locked brothers up by the boatload for selling it. Subpar educations, hopelessness, and high unemployment set the stage for plenty of Black men to see no other way to subsist. Until 2010, crack fetched 100 times more prison time than its powdered form. Crack continues to be the drug most often sold and consumed in poor predominantly Black communities. President Obama reduced the cocaine/crack punishment disparity to 18 to 1 with the Fair Sentencing Act. Up until that time, sentences for offenses involving crack cocaine averaged 100 times longer time in prison than those for the sentences involving powder cocaine. Even with that change,18 to 1 still represents a very racist disparity. People of color receive (10%) longer prison sentences than Whites in the federal court system. For identical convictions, mandatory minimums are handed out to Blacks (21%) more.

CHAPTER 22
The Beautiful Struggle

Black Hip Hop fans never demanded from our artists that they ramp up the crime, drugs, murder, and misogyny in Hip Hop. That decision came from the top. The only reason music glorifying negativity is outselling conscious Hip Hop is because the negative variety receives far more exposure and financial backing from those who now own Hip Hop, not us. Please feel free to draw your own conclusions in regard to why the powers that be decided that messages that uplift, inspire, and empower should take a back seat to music that inspires Black children to be less than who they're capable. We are living the manifestations daily. When both conscious Hip Hop and Gangster Rap are juxtaposed, talent is a much better indicator of success than content. Sadly, today's urban radio formats don't give the listeners options beyond what can be termed "genocide music". Listeners have illusory choices between artists with very marginal talent. One of the newer rappers recently stated in so many words that lyrics aren't important anymore in Hip Hop. Never thought I'd see the day. There was a time when the actual Hip Hop community, the artists, decided who qualified, and who should be ostracized and crucified, never to pick up a microphone again. Today, those decisions are being made by whiter higher ups who fish through YouTube looking for the next Black pusher to promote negative propaganda to Black youth. They're a dime a dozen. Talent isn't required. Just spit what's on the template and collect a bag of money. When Black youth were held by the Hip Hop community to produce a higher standard, the bar was constantly raised, genius and creativity ruled. Now that individuals from beyond the threshold of the culture are making those decisions, the bar is as low as it's ever been. I blame the industry because I know what Black youth are capable of without anti-culture controls and constraints. It takes a village.

Again, we're engaged in a war for the minds of our youth. It's important that we understand this. As stated earlier, there has been no time in America when America wasn't targeting us for disrespect or death. It's the distractions that lead us to forget. We need to hold our young responsible to our community and our culture, but more importantly, we need to target those entities that target us. Why are Blacks in America the only race that gets to be called the disgusting term attached to their debasement? Why do we never get to hear the words, "Hymie", "Heeb", or "Kike" employed by music artists? The rapper Drake has a father who is Black and a mother who is Jewish. Why is he so comfortable referring to Black men as niggas and Black women as bitches but never making use of such colorful language to defame his mother's heritage? No other race on the planet gets to be disrespected with vile terminology via mainstream media every hour of the day. Just us. Still nigga?? NEVER nigga. We are AFRICANS.

Not too long ago, there was a video of the young rapper, Bobby Shmurda, dancing on a table in a record company office for a record contract. The audition was mostly painfully contrived dance moves and barely audible mumbling. There were about 20 people in the room, with the majority being White. There were only a few Blacks in the room watching Shmurda do his best "buck dance for bucks". One of those people was Epic Records executive, LA Reid. It was difficult to watch and appeared very awkward. That spectacle was reminiscent of the minstrel shows Blacks were forced to partake in to get into showbiz. We didn't own the mediums then and we don't own them now. I guess we get what we get until we decide to demand more. Until then, the minstrel shows continue. Black culture with the culture erased. Blackface.

MOVING FORWARD

One cannot present solutions without first evidencing an understanding of the problems at hand. Balance is a penchant for acknowledging problems but also the willingness and ability to offer viable solutions to address them. The incessant problem peddler eventually discredits him/herself serving as the sensationalist cynic who profits from constantly airing the negative. This is the America's news and social media platforms. There's money to be made and attention to be garnered through the constant promotion of unfortunate events and people. Progress is understanding the problems, mining the solutions, and then applying those solutions.

As a Black teacher of the Social Sciences, Media, and Consumer Education, I have always felt the obligation to impart information to Black students that they are rarely taught in America's public schools. I've accomplished this within the constraints of working in schools and beyond them, conducting workshops as a guest in different schools and at community centers. I've come to value these conversations among and amidst vested community members that deal with the real issues, sans a state-mandated curriculum, state-minded employers, and state defined benchmark assessments. My focus in my presentations has always been Media Literacy, the purpose and uses of media and its effects on our thoughts and behaviors. For me, it's easy to teach Media Literacy within the context of Hip Hop because as a culture, Hip Hop has permeated every medium this country utilizes. Very potent messages are delivered to the consumers via artists who promote messages that lift the community up and those who promote what lowers our collective vibration. The latter purvey what aligns perfectly with destructive agendas that have been in play for quite some time. The subject of Hip Hop provides the perfect springboard for conversations about propaganda and how it's used to manipulate how people think and what and when they think about it. Among the most potent parts of any culture is its music. Hip Hop is a huge piece of who we are, it defines our youth in many regards. Hip Hop was co-opted, corrupted, repackaged, and sold to us as Black culture through media we consume daily. We bought it. I've learned a lot conducting the workshops and they've generally been mutually enriching. I've always felt I could and should do more though.

ORGANIZING

Some years ago, I had the good fortune of participating in a meeting that was convened in a coffee shop on the south side of Chicago to deal with the media's attacks on Black culture and Black children. There were about ten of us in attendance. We never settled on a cohesive and sustained course of action after several meetings, but I was able to maintain contact with a brother, Kwabena Rasuli of the Clear the Airwaves Project. He invited me to protests of urban radio stations and actions targeting the sponsors of these radio stations. Kwabena and his group had already seen some success with the Clear the Airwaves Project in Indiana. They were able to get a local Menard's hardware store to pull advertising from Hammond, Indiana's Power 92.3 WPWX, a station that featured that ubiquitous urban death soundtrack iHeartRadio and Crawford Communications like to target Black youth with. I stood with the Clear the Airwaves Project for over a year almost every weekend on the south side of Chicago in front of a McDonalds restaurant. We opted to protest in front of McDonald's in Chicago's Woodlawn community because McDonald's is a major sponsor on both major radio stations in Chicago that feature Black sonic self-destruction. Notable is the fact that this particular McDonald's is the first Black-owned McDonald's in the country. Its owner is also a member of the BMOA (Black McDonalds Owners Association). We met a lot of good and interested people, young and old, on those Saturday mornings. Most importantly, we were able to call attention to the issue of the music and the radio stations. Eventually, Kwabena, through some contacts, got us a meeting with Clear Channel (now iHeart Communications) which is located in Chicago's downtown area. The meeting began and ended contentiously with the general manager at the time, Earl Jones, a Black man, refusing to yield on the negative messaging in the music. He eventually kicking us out of the radio station after attempting to woo us with some weak concessions, seats at tables where Black people don't eat. He had his orders and he was unwilling to step out of line. We left Clear Channel's Chicago office with a clearer understanding of the work that lied ahead.

Kwabena remains the face and the feet of the Clear the Airwaves Project and he eventually connected us with a group of elders in New York who were serious about taking back what is ours, Black culture. We attended a meeting in Harlem, New York in March of 2017 where several important issues relative to Black progress in America were discussed. The goal was to not only cover the problems relevant to the Black community, but also to help map out action-oriented solutions moving forward. Legendary radio personality and activist, Bob Law, was the meeting's facilitator. The Clear the Airwaves Project joined with the National Black Leadership Alliance (NBLA), an organization that had been in existence for a few years. By the end of the meeting, it was decided that we needed to be working both diligently and purposefully towards addressing four major components: education, culture, politics, and economics. These are the pillars we identified as solid foundational items to build upon. Every Thursday evening, without fail, a conference call is held to discuss what's occurring within each of these four societal components and what actions are taking place to address them. The following is a summary of relevant issues, observations, and needed courses of action from my personal vantage, as well as courses of action being undertaken through the Clear the Airwaves Project and the National Black Leadership Alliance.

1. Education

"Only a fool would let his enemy teach his children"

- Malcolm X -

For far too long, we've been content to allow our children to matriculate through schools that do not empower them. At the most, America's public schools offer us the opportunity to earn degrees that allow access to employment. Since inception, the schools mostly attended by Black children have served the unexpressed goals of Black assimilation, integration, and enculturation. This is done through Euro-centered curricula that distorts and dismisses Black culture; Black accomplishments, real Black history, and real Black heroes. By the time the average Black kid has graduated from college, he or she is tooled with just enough information to fulfill the requirements of a job, but too often doesn't possess a knowledge and love of self that would lend to any meaningful and sustained Black community advocacy. We become great consumers but are far less likely to meet the production and creation needs within our own communities. We're all familiar with the school-to-prison pipeline that sees many of our children either dropping out or disconnecting mentally from the educational process in a way that breeds menial existences, criminal involvement, or proxy suicidal behavior. Many Black communities are struggling because of both failing schools that succeed in maintaining the status quo and the intentional lack of employment opportunities.

The situation is growing worse with the advent of charter schools. Charter schools are privatized profit-driven entities. Charter school proliferation is occurring in mostly communities of Black and Brown children across America. At the same time, public schools within these communities are shuttered and closed down, long ago set up to fail. Many of these charters are directly connected to corporate interests and therefore feature curricula in line with those same interests. Charter schools feature the dissolution of teacher unions and the depression of teacher salaries and benefits. Teacher certification isn't a requirement in many of them. In terms of staffing, they tend to weed out Black veteran professional educators while opening the door for younger teachers unfamiliar with or unwilling to adapt to the cultures, environments, or realities of Black students. Both public schools and public charter schools in urban areas around the nation have seen their arts and vocational programs whittled away to make way for massive standardized test preparation which just happens to be profit driven. There seems to be a new test, a new way to teach the test, or a new way to teach teachers how to teach the test every couple of years. The goal never seems to be real education.

Black children aren't being educated, they continue to be subjected to intense indoctrination.

NBLA's focus, in this vein, is to help fund and eventually help cultivate independent Afro-Centered schools. NBLA has started the GRACE fund which helps pool money for independent Afro-centered schools already in existence. GRACE stands for "granting resources and cultivating excellence". The NBLA utilizes multiple social media platforms and fundraising to collect monies to help sustain these schools and hopefully see them grow. No child is truly educated until they know themselves, their history, and their own culture. Independent Afro-Centered schools help foster a strong sense of pride and self-esteem in Black children. A potent Afro-Centered education helps motivate Black children who want to become entrepreneurs and business owners. Most importantly, these schools help to cultivate Black leaders. Please consider visiting GRACE's GoFundMe page for more information about the fund and consider a donation to NBLA's efforts to help support schools that empower Black children.
https://www.gofundme.com/GRACEEDUFUND

2. Culture

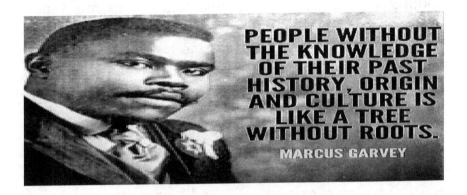

PEOPLE WITHOUT THE KNOWLEDGE OF THEIR PAST HISTORY, ORIGIN AND CULTURE IS LIKE A TREE WITHOUT ROOTS.
MARCUS GARVEY

The culture of a people is the collective expression of their collective consciousness. This expression reflects their shared past. The modes of expression commonly associated with culture are thoughts, ideas, art, literature, and normalized behaviors.

African people are a very expressive people. A major conduit for Black expression has always been our art. Our music has historically been used to convey strong emotions and meaningful messages. African drums have always been critical for African people. They provided our ceremonial soundtracks and were also a means of conveying covert escape plans during chattel slavery. When we are in control of our own musical expressions, the messages cover the spectrum of our existence as whole people. We are multi-faceted, and we have been and are a great many things. We are gods, goddesses, kings, queens, brothers, sisters, inventors, creators, and lovers. At the same time, our existence in this country sees us being able to identify with the more carnal as well. We have our issues.

If someone unfamiliar with Black people and Black culture was exposed to a few hours of urban radio and about a day's worth of BET, what conclusions could they draw about Black people? What are the prevailing messages and themes? As it stands, Black people in America don't own the mediums that promote our images, narratives, and stories. As a result, the majority of the time Blacks are portrayed as criminals, murderers, thugs, drug dealers, drug addicts, subservient slaves, niggas, bitches, thots, hoes, materialistic shallow morons, ignorant, one-dimensional, uneducated, listless, lazy, wayward, over-sexualized, and worthy of being euthanized. These depictions are very functional. They are key to maintaining the status quo. In order to keep us in last place, it's important that we're constantly portrayed as deserving of that position.

We need to be combating these negative propaganda campaigns targeting us. More importantly, we need to be erecting mediums to distribute our own images, narratives, and stories. At this juncture, it would be silly to expect our historical enemies to portray us in a positive light. We constantly expose their efforts to defame us as we build our own platforms. We must call attention to toxic propaganda and its effects. Simultaneously, we need to promote those artists and others who speak life into our people. We need to recognize and reward them. NBLA is about creating our own propaganda campaigns to portray who we truly are, not the caricatures created by American media. Black people love one another and there are plenty of Black relationships and marriages that reflect this truth. Black people have a very rich history and culture that embraces love, respect, principles, integrity, and honor.

A Historical & Sociological Perspective

We have a glorious history and ancestry saturated with greatness. We've always had musical artists who created music genres and conveyed some of the deepest social, political, and emotional messages through innate artistic talent. We are born with it; we just need to cultivate and nourish it. Most times, the myriad of artistic talents our children are born with wind up lying dormant throughout their entire lives. Their gifts are never accessed or tapped into due to educational processes that don't lend to self-discovery. We just need to show Black children who they are, the rest comes naturally. NBLA will help build Black media platforms and will continue to help promote the very positive aspects of Black culture. We have an abundance.

3. Politics

VOTE NOV 5TH
HUEY NEWTON
FOR U.S. CONGRESS

DEFEND THE BLACK COMMUNITY
AND THE PEOPLE'S HUMAN RIGHTS
HUEY NEWTON'S name will be on the Nov 5th Ballot as Candidate for the 7th C.D.
ALL POWER TO ALL THE PEOPLE
BLACK POWER TO BLACK PEOPLE

Co-founder of the Black Panther Party, Huey Newton, made an unsuccessful bid for U.S. Congress in 1968 on the "Peace and Freedom Party" ticket. (HA.com, Heritage Auctions, 2019)

When Blacks gave 80% of our votes to the Democratic Party in 1964, Black activist Malcolm X appropriately labeled us "political chumps."

Obama garnered (96%) of the Black vote in 2007, and then (93%) in 2011. We expected and received relatively nothing during his tenure in office. In many regards, we lost ground. Blacks lost wealth, homes, and our communities continued to hemorrhage Black lives, much of that attrition attributed to state-sanctioned authority. Around the globe, Africans continued to feel the wrath of America's Draconian foreign policies.

As President, Obama behaved like an enemy of Africa. He oversaw the assassination of Muammar Gaddafi. Gaddafi was a staunch Pan-Africanist who sought a United African Union. His assassination during Obama's tenure set the African continent back decades. At the same time, Obama drone bombed African countries into oblivion. The lives of innocent Black men, women, and children chalked up as collateral. Obama's platform saw him continuing to mainline money into Israel to the tune of billions as Israel oppressed and murdered many of its African minority. The United States military continued to plunder Africa. AFRICOM (the United States Africa Command) was established in Ghana, reinforcing America's neo-colonist ties to the continent. The 44th President proved that the title, "Nobel Peace Prize Winner" was just a label.

Obama undermined efforts to combat police brutality. He played the fence when it came time to call out the fact that White police officers were lynching Black people with lead launchers. He directed his ire at the young Black men in Baltimore angrily protesting the killing of Freddie Gray. He labeled them "criminals and thugs' but was measured in his words for the Baltimore police officers solely responsible for Mr. Gray's back being broken into two pieces in the back of a police vehicle. The Black youth, especially those experiencing certain urban realities daily, realize that peaceful protests often come off as impotence. Sometimes, you have to tear down that fence. There has never been a peaceful revolution in the history of the world.

Obama's advocacy for Blacks in America left a lot to be desired. He allowed the corrupt convict bankers who functionally killed the U.S. economy at the beginning of his first term to skate free, unscathed. The stock market crash of 2008 negatively impacted Black people both socially and economically. What relatively little wealth Blacks possessed evaporated. He bailed out financial entities that had economically exploited Blacks, padding the pockets of greedy CEOs with billions. Meanwhile, he declared that reparations for the multiple centuries of Black enslavement and oppression was unfeasible. Black educators and children began feeling it with Bush's *No Child Left Behind* and saw many of the same debilitating policies continued through Obama's *Race to The Top*. He oversaw and helped shepherd the proliferation of charter schools in Black communities, costing many Black teachers their sanity and careers, while crippling Black students and helping to further destabilize Black communities. He flew into Chicago twice to campaign for a racist mayor who continued to make life for Chicago's Black community miserable. Black people gained nothing for having a Black President in the Oval Office for 8 years.

Obama has a silky-smooth knack for appealing to both the Black "exceptional" and the Black poor while doing nothing for the latter and only serving up the symbolic to the former. The image of Obama and his family was powerful, the substance we needed just never made it to the table. Obama did his job as most U.S. Presidents do, adhering to both America's longstanding foreign and domestic policies. Neither of those robust policy platforms have ever featured advocacy for America's Black constituents or our family around the globe. We hoped though. We surrendered almost 100% of our votes to Obama but never felt the inclination to hold him accountable to us. He stuck to the script and we were enamored by his performance. We can't continue to throw our love and support behind politicians simply based on them being Black and Democratic.

We have to stop being the political chumps Malcolm X referred to. Voting for us has to become a lot more than sitting around waiting until election day and voting on the corporate-funded Democrats and Republicans provided to us, the illusion of choices. We have to begin to wield our considerable collective voting power in a manner that sees us being acknowledged after all of the votes have been counted and not just when it's time to campaign in Black churches or pose with Black children. No more being pawns.

Voting intelligently is participation throughout the entire political process from beginning to end. We have to organize and craft political agendas and platforms that speak to what our immediate community needs are. Start with local elections and form voting blocs centered around our demands. Cultivate, fund, and support candidates from within our communities who have shown a history of meaningful community advocacy. Arm these candidates with the platforms and agendas that we've crafted to a progressive consensus and hold them accountable for following through on our demands. Support candidates who aren't beholden to political machines. Be aware of referendums, recalls, and matters on the ballot besides the actual candidates. Vote with our pertinent issues in mind and not the influence of media-fueled popularity and propaganda. We have to get to the point where we're seeing beyond the sound bites and talking points of news pundits and polished politicians. Everything must be subject to critical analysis, not the continued exploitation of our emotions.

Our historical reality has featured most politicians, even the ones who look like us, not truly being interested or vested in any real policies or actions that have brought about any real changes in the Black community. Most of them have been purchased by corporate or political entities; they no longer belong to us. The status quo hasn't changed, and the Black collective has continued to cling to that bottom rung. We've been voting for about 50 years and we've had hundreds of Black politicians in key offices, even the Oval Office. With that said, we have to remain involved. Laws and policies do affect us, and we can't afford to surrender our political power for political passivity. The key is to participate from an informed position and to couple that participation with real community activism. Voting, by itself, doesn't qualify as activism, and our great ancestry didn't struggle, fight, and die for us to cast a ballot. They died for us to be free. We don't have time to be comfortable or complacent. There is plenty of work to do. Respect, love, and honor for our ancestry who helped get us this far.

4. Economics

I do not want to lend credence to what exist, but reality is we live within a capitalist structure and until we change that, we must find a way to maneuver within it. We have to play the game while working to defeat it and ultimately destroy it. The goal is to maneuver within it in a manner that benefits our collective until we can free ourselves from it. Our dilemma and contradiction is starving the beast while feeding it.

Any in-depth analysis will reveal that there is no such thing as an altruistic or humanitarian version of capitalism. It's an intrinsically evil ideology. The Cold War featured a series of wars in Asia where millions of soldiers and civilians were killed, all in the name of containing communism, and as a corollary, clearing the way for the spread of capitalism. If capitalism was a real benefit to humanity, there'd be no need to kill in order to employ it, for us to enjoy it. There is no "good capitalism". It is a totally profit-driven economic system, a monstrosity of a machine. There are a few winners and an entire world of losers. Ecosystems, people, trees, plants, animals, the atmosphere, and entire bodies of water are exploited to see a relative few entrenched in the black.

Humans are utilized as resources and programmed as automatons who accept this existence. Our entire public-school system, with its adeptness at creating standardized worker bees and not those who control their own means of subsistence, is a key component. The prison and military industrial complexes are cruel creations of capitalism. A healthcare industry that focuses on treatment versus prevention is a sick manifestation of capitalism. The inclination to enslave and own human beings is among the most egregious manifestations of an ideology that continuously places profits over people. Debt and wage peonage are capitalism's main cogs. Capitalism's greatest con is being able to convince people that it is a gift to humanity, all while bringing out the worst in human beings. We are all primed to consume.

As Black people in America, not only have we been primed to consume, but we've been primed to consume against our own interests and in the interests of everyone else. This isn't a genetic disorder, but the direct result of our adaptation here. Media drives our lust to consume and America's schools do not cultivate the mind that critically analyzes information imparted to us. Media helps create mindsets where we attach status and success to our ability to consume, to have access to the "finer things". I've been there. Don't get me wrong, this isn't just a Black thing, this illness is manifested across the board with all of America's impressionable. What negatively impacts most Americans is critical to us based on our lack of power; we don't have the luxury of apathy. We have to curb our mindless consumption, if not for our own community, for the sake of the planet, both intrinsically intertwined.

Our exceptional matriculate through schools and receive degrees that enable them to work jobs that afford them the ability to buy houses, cars, and send their children away to school. However, even among the exceptional, one quick downward market trend can easily dissolve whatever wealth we've collectively accrued. Our homes are easily devalued through recessions and racist urban policies. We've witnessed this. We're economically vulnerable. That vulnerability is founded in the fact that we reside in neighborhoods we do not own.

Ownership encompasses owning the banks, grocery stores, schools, and other institutions a group of people rely on to survive. We are far less economically vulnerable when we own our own banks. Owning our own financial institutions would certainly prevent our being discriminated against and being denied home/business loans. We'd less likely be extended predatory loans at inflated interest rates. It is far easier to build as a community when we own the establishments within our communities that enable us to employ our people and our children who need means of subsistence or apprenticeships. We need to own and control our schools and install curricula that tools our children to grow their own food, build homes, become plumbers and electricians, become artists, and the entrepreneurs our communities need. We need financial literacy that teaches empowerment through production/creation versus frivolous consumption. African children require an Afro-centered education in order to be empowered. At the end of the day, Black teachers need to be teaching the realities of capitalism to Black students in a manner that grooms them to push for far greater later down the line. Our struggle isn't just about race.

We have to learn the meaning of divesting. To divest means to deprive of power. We give our power away to other people every time we give our money to them. Our communities are stocked with gas stations, grocery stores, banks, beauty supply stores, and eateries that belong to other people. We enrich them and thereby help enrich their communities. They contribute nothing to ours. When we venture into their communities, we don't find Black-owned businesses. They won't allow it. Why do we allow them to prey on us so indiscriminately? We can build everything we need for ourselves. We have a lengthy history of autonomy, time to go back to basics.

We need to become consumers who support Black businesses as habit, survival, and out of a genuine love for Black people. There are plenty of Black business owners who are looking to grow and there are those that have been long-established. The more they grow, we all do. The bigger they grow, the more of us they can employ. Black businesses need to form those chambers of commerce or incubators that facilitate the growth of other businesses while creating a resource pool for themselves and finding/funding ways to support the surrounding community. Support those Black businesses that support the Black community, not just those who linger within our communities and take our money for granted. A parasitic mindset only recognizes the color green. It is important we recognize and celebrate those Black business owners who genuinely care about the community. Black-owned businesses are essential. We can't keep hemorrhaging all of our community's talent and money.

It's crucial that we have educators who help mold students who are uninterested in defining themselves based on how much they can spend and what unnecessary, fleeting, and depreciating material goods they can accumulate. If we focused our spending inwardly instead of outwardly, we'd already be where we need to be. I am sure many of us have allowed ourselves to be sucked into bad consumerist habits because of Western media and the associated socialization. There is no way our children should grow up looking forward to being able to throw money at Gucci, Fendi, Chanel, Louis Vuitton, Tom Ford. or any of these over-priced, inflated value items we're trained to love. Again, this isn't just a Black thing, this is so very American, but again, as a collective, we can't afford it. We've been socialized to assign value to material items that intrinsically possess none. Would any of us pay $500 for a belt that features a local stranger's initials on a leather strap? What are our initials worth on that same belt? Why are Guccio Gucci's initials magnets for our money? Funny thing is, most of these Italian fashion houses bit our style long ago and have continued to siphon style from us. What's stopping us from building our own fashion houses? We need to continue to support those who are doing just that. We must make certain we are building the entities to provide our children with the opportunities to learn how to become designers of their own clothing. Italy doesn't care about Black communities here in America. Why are we so happy to contribute to theirs? Our spending habits are a direct reflection of both our self-love and our self-loathing. Our survival depends on us feeding ourselves.

Diamonds for What?

The diamond industry has been conning us forever. DeBeers hooked Europe, America, Japan, and many other Westernized regions on the idea that the union between a man and woman must be preceded by the purchase of an expensive rock. Since 1938, DeBeers has been pouring money into campaigns to pull hard-earned wages out of men's pockets to establish their worth with a woman. Cecil Rhodes was the racist imperialist who founded the DeBeers diamond company. The DeBeers company had control of global distribution until the 21st century. His control of large swaths of land in Africa saw millions of Africans enslaved and murdered for his company to grow. Rhodes has an Oxford University scholarship named for him, the Rhodes Scholarship. Two African countries, Zimbabwe and Zambia, used to be named for him. They were previously Northern and Southern Rhodesia. His company made a mint convincing the entire globe that diamonds are precious and rare. Diamonds are not rare, they are quite plentiful, and they aren't worth anywhere near 3 months wages. However, that's what we've been repeatedly told. Once an act has been branded tradition, it becomes an automatic behavior, a ritual, and the consensus expectation. Late night cartoons tend to contain more potent social commentary than an entire day's worth of corporate news programming

A Historical & Sociological Perspective

Rick and Morty cartoon excerpt

Jerry: "Traditionally, science fairs are a father-son thing."

Rick: "Well, scientifically speaking, traditions are an idiot thing."

I don't dislike traditions; I actually see some value in them. There is some validity to what the overly cynical cartoon character, Rick, posits. Traditions are beliefs and customs that have been passed down from generation to generation. Traditions usually have a cultural component. Being a component of the culture within which that tradition exists, the expectation is that the tradition possesses some intrinsic value that continually enriches the culture that hosts it. Otherwise, why pass it down? Why promote it? The empty tradition of purchasing diamond rings as a preface to matrimony is an American tradition, a very capitalist one. It has absolutely nothing to do with Black culture or Black love. It plays no real part in the unions of any ethnic group either beyond being a predatory tradition that we were all socialized to accept, hollow symbolism. The tradition of spending thousands of dollars on ring mounted rocks doesn't benefit us and, in many ways, it hurts us economically. Our blind acceptance of this tradition benefits those who implanted the idea back in 1938 through well-placed advertising. These are the same people who seek to exterminate as many Africans as possible in their conquest of the African continent and the abundant resources it holds.

Through well thought out ad campaigns, companies convince Americans to consume what they don't have a true need for. Advertisers implant ideas into our minds which they nourish through repetition and appeals to our egos and emotions. All that's required is 3 minutes of research and an open mind to become an individual who sees most of these cons for what they are. The diamond industry and many others are the continuation of Africa's exploitation by Europeans; maximized extraction. What if the curricula in America's schools tooled students to think for themselves? As adults who have the obligation of seeing our seeds evolve to be far better than us, we have to understand that it starts with us. We can't expect our children to be better and do better if we're saddling them with the exact same alien beliefs and traditions we were indoctrinated with. Let the next generation evolve. Many of us say we want change, but don't actually want to change. We want to talk about how awful the world is and how things need to change for the better, but we're often unwilling to even consider the tiniest of adjustments within ourselves. Africans on every continent are connected and our mistreatment anywhere binds us all too common pain, the same oppression. We need to minimize our complicity. We need to begin to act as a community.

A Historical & Sociological Perspective

Diamond Child Labour (Youtu.be/m7isPiZCe84, 2016)

Many of us lament about the practice of selling human beings into slavery that still goes on in Africa and other places. We bitch, moan, and post on our social media about how unjust and inhumane it is. But then we go mute when we receive information about how the diamond industry employs child labor in Africa and how dangerous diamond mines lead to the deaths of many African people. Our African brothers and sisters don't matter to us when it's time to engage our Western assimilation. I wore diamonds earrings as a young man. I bought watches that contained diamonds, flossing but hardly bossing. The only thing I can contribute those purchases to was profound ignorance. I didn't know any better. When presented with the information, I made the adjustment. It was not difficult. I asked myself, "what are some of the things of value I can dedicate my hard-earned money to instead of valueless, rapidly depreciating stones that enrich a racist industry?" I immediately think of King Leopold and Cecil Rhodes when I see diamonds. Read about the genocidal campaigns carried out by each and you'll understand how backwards it is for an African or anyone of African descent to support the diamond industry. They killed millions of African people, stole their land, and then started DeBeers. As a company, DeBeers would amputate the limbs of African children when the children did not meet quotas set by their DeBeers bosses. As men, try to be more creative and imaginative with your marriage proposals. True love has absolutely nothing to do with an expensive, hyper-depreciating piece of jewelry, it absolutely does not. Women, please try to see things for what they are. Respect the man who is willing to do it differently out of respect for our distant family. The hope is that when I decide to marry, it'll be with someone who has committed to some of the same changes I'm trying to make, especially in regard to purchasing diamonds. If the woman I seek wouldn't prefer to buy land or build some businesses together instead, we probably aren't "evenly yoked" to begin with. On to another egg.

Gradually, we must remove our consumption from the diamond industry. We must also disengage from many other industries that exploit our immense collective resources and economic immaturity. Much of what we consume has its origin in some region or country Europe or America is exploiting for its natural or human resources. Living here in America, it's almost impossible to completely end our complicity to this dynamic, but we can certainly work to minimize our involvement.

Heart Work

Black men and women, we have plenty of room to grow. It's obvious we can't continue as is and expect to win as a collective. I employ the word collective a lot because it is the mode we need to engage in order to function effectively. Sure, some of us are making good money and living well within the context of capitalism. However, as a collective, we are not winning. There are no winners on a team in last place. It's that much more difficult to win when members of our team don't understand that we're behind in the score. There are too many focused on their own individual stats, personal glory. These disconnected individuals tend to operate in their own self-interests.

They do not see a collective unless they are joltingly reminded which team they're on by the opposing team. Some do not claim a collective until they're faced with the reality Dr. Clarke spoke of when he stated, "the African has no friends". The hope is that it does not require a traumatic wake-up call to serve as a reminder that all of us need all of us. We need to educate our own children for empowerment. We need to wield our own culture as a tool to define ourselves. We need to engage politics that result in relevant, sustainable advocacy. In addition, we need to resort to consuming in a manner that reflects a love for ourselves. We have a way to go but we can get there. We just have to want to. We have a multitude of precedents of African greatness.

We had ancestry who built civilizations on every continent. We managed to build thriving, autonomous communities in America despite several centuries of hell. We've gifted America our gifts and talents, mostly unacknowledged, all exploited for America's benefit, not our own. Our goal isn't to come to a place we haven't previously been, it's simply to get back to being where we were, to get back to being ourselves. We absolutely have everything we need among ourselves. As a collective, we have to change. As individuals, we have to change. At this juncture, we can't concern ourselves with a few "bad apples", we have enough onboard to move forward and we will. I see shining examples of Black greatness daily, and I know plenty of Black youth who reassure me that our future is in good hands, we just need to continue to cultivate them so they may cultivate others, dutiful dominoes.

A Historical & Sociological Perspective

Hip Hop is a portrait of us. Greatness, genius, and creativity. Our existence in America has seen us controlled and owned by others, eventually diluted to where we were no longer recognizable beyond outer-appearance, shells of our former selves, shell-shocked. We were distorted into what those who captured us needed us to be in order for them to exploit us, in order for them to dominate and subjugate us. We've appeared as corrupted and compromised, well-socialized. Hip Hop as commercialized. However, darkness can't conceal light for long. We are the original children of the sun; we came after no one. We are awakening from our slumber. We will rise. We will walk again as the potent force we were prior to being encroached upon by savagery. We are Hip Hop. Hip Hop isn't going anywhere, and neither are we. Our culture is ours to reclaim. The struggle of our ancestry will not be in vain.

Ase

Easy Advocacy

As a concerned member of the community, you can contact the FCC (Federal Communications Commission) regarding the obscenity these European-owned urban radio stations continuously target Black children with.

What is obscene?

Obscene material is not protected by the 1st Amendment of the Constitution and cannot be broadcast at any time. The Supreme Court has established that in order to be considered obscene, material must meet a three-pronged test:

- an average person, applying contemporary community standards, must find that the material, as a whole, appeals to the prurient interests.

- the material must depict or describe, in a patently offensive way, sexual conduct specifically defined by applicable law.

- the material, taken as a whole, must lack serious literary, artistic, political, or scientific value.

What qualifies as a violation?

It is a violation of federal law to air obscene programming at any time or indecent programming or profane language from 6AM to 10PM. Congress has given the FCC the responsibility for administratively enforcing these laws. The FCC may revoke a station license, impose a monetary forfeiture, or issue a warning if a station airs obscene, indecent or profane material.

Contact the FCC:

http://consumercomplaints.fcc.gov/hc/en-us/articles/202731600-obscene-indecent-and-profane-broadcasts

Organizations Addressing Toxic Media Targeting African People:

Clear the Airwaves Project - Chicago/Gary/Dallas

National Black Leadership Alliance (NBLA)

Rage Against the Ratchet - Philadelphia

Committee to Eliminate Media Offensive to Afrikan People

(CEMOTAP) – New York/Los Angeles

National Congress of Black Women – Washington, DC

Please Understand

"When you control opinion, as corporate America controls opinion in the United States by owning the media, you can make the masses believe almost anything you want and guide them as you please."

- Gore Vidal -

wake up!

ACKNOWLEDGMENTS

Thank you, Bernard Creamer Sr. and Pamela Y. Creamer, for your discipline, nurturance, and tolerance. I could not ask for a better beginning. Thank you to my sister, Lisa Creamer, for always being there. Thank you, Darrin and Devin (and now Carter too!), for allowing me to enter your lives late in the game; I couldn't be prouder. Thank you extended family and friends. Special thanks to Dr. Lance Williams for opening my eyes to the fact that they were closed years ago. Special thanks to all of those who have helped bridge my transitions financially and emotionally; I love and appreciate you. Much love and respect to our esteemed and honorable ancestry who did the work that allows us to continue the work. Lastly, thank you to the vanguard of rarely acknowledged sisters and brothers who continue to struggle against the status quo and for the minds infected by it. As one people, we can accomplish everything. FORWARD

Printed in the USA
CPSIA information can be obtained
at www.ICGtesting.com
LVHW010434291223
767710LV00003B/96